Facing the Future

D1235953

David Spangler

Facing the Future

Edited by Julia Spangler
Book Design by Jeremy Berg
Cover and Interior Photos from istockphoto

Published by Lorian Press
2204 E Grand Ave.
Everett, WA 98201

ISBN-10: 0-936878-28-2
ISBN-13: 978-0-936878-28-7

Spangler/David
Facing the Future/David Spangler

First Edition March 2010

Printed in the United States of America

0 9 8 7 6 5 4 3 2 1

www.lorian.org

Dedication

I dedicate this book to all who are working to ensure that
Humanity has a future that is bountiful, blessed, connected
to the world, and always evolving.

David Spangler Books

Subtle Worlds: *An Explorer's Field Notes*

Blessing: *The Art and the Practice*

The Call

Parent as Mystic - Mystic as Parent

Manifestation: *Creating the life you love*

Everyday Miracles

The Laws of Manifestation

The Story Tree

The Incarnational Card Deck and Manual

The Flame of Incarnation

Lorian Textbook Series

World Work

Crafting Home: *Generating the Sacred*

Space-Crafting: *The Holding of Self*

Crafting Relationships: *The Holding of Others*

Crafting Inner Alliances: *The Holding of Spirit*

Incarnational Spirituality: *A strategy to Bless our World*

Acknowledgements

As I've said at other times, a book is always the product of many minds, many hearts, and many hands. I want to acknowledge and thank those who made this book possible. Chief among these is my wife, Julie, with whom I am proud and delighted to be facing the future. I could not ask for a better partner. Plus she is my main editor, making this, like all my books, better than it would have been otherwise.

I want to acknowledge my partners in Lorian Jeremy Berg and Freya Secrest, also without whom this book would not be here. I could not ask for better friends or colleagues. This is especially true as Jeremy is my publisher as well as my friend. Once again, thank, you, Jeremy, for the outstanding cover!

I want to thank all those who participated in my Path of the Self class, as part of the Path of the Chalice program. They let me disappear from their midst for a week while I finished this manuscript. I owe them!

And finally—and very far from least—I wish to acknowledge and thank all those who are working to define and shape our future, the men and women whose books and websites I reference in the Resources section of this book. I owe all of you a debt as well for your wisdom, your thoughts, your visions, and your courage.

Table of Contents

Chapter One: A Time of Change 1

Chapter Two: The Apocalyptic Imagination 7

Chapter Three: Visions of Utopia 17

Chapter Four: Falling from the Trampoline 29

Chapter Five: The Three Futures 41

Chapter Six: Miracles 51

Chapter Seven: An Ecology of Time 61

Chapter Eight: Invisible Friends 73

Chapter Nine: Consciousness 87

Chapter Ten: Star Power 99

Chapter Eleven: Facing the Future 109

Chapter Twelve: Engaging the Future 127

Chapter Thirteen: Day by Day 143

Chapter Fourteen: School Kids 151

Resources i

Chapter One
A Time of Change

When I was a child in the nineteen-fifties, the future was well laid out. Articles in glossy magazines like the *Saturday Evening Post* and *Life Magazine* told the story in glorious detail with pictures that thoroughly captured my imagination. By the year 2000 C.E. there would be space travel, of course, with space stations around the earth and colonies on the moon and Mars. Nuclear power would give us unlimited energy. We would all be flying about in family air cars, hovercraft and personal jet packs. Diseases would be eliminated or nearly so. Robots would be everywhere doing all the chores and manual labor. There were never any poor people in the magazine illustrations (for that matter, there were never any persons of color either...the future seemed entirely made up of Anglo-Americans). When I was thirteen in 1958, I was chosen to be Valedictorian for my grade school graduating class. I gave my talk on scientific progress and the advances in technology that we could expect to see in our lifetime, all inspired by these wonderful articles.

Of course, the future wasn't all bright and shiny. Lurking in the background was the specter of nuclear war and the death of civilization. As it happened, I grew up in North Africa where my father, a military man, was stationed on an American air base for several years. As a consequence I missed a lot of the fear that inspired suburbanites to build fallout shelters in their backyards or school children to duck under their desks during nuclear air raid drills, as if kneeling under a few inches of wood would protect them from the effects of blast and radiation. I don't remember us ever having such drills. I suspect that because we were living on a Strategic Air Command base where, rumor had it, the bombers were armed with atomic bombs, everyone knew we were a prime target and that no amount of drilling could protect us if we were ground zero for a nuclear blast.

As it turned out, that nuclear holocaust never occurred. But then, neither did that bright technological future of robots and jet packs that my friends and I had taken for granted in the Fifties. The articles were wrong. Here we are in 2010 and there are no colonies on other worlds. There's an International Space Station but it's a pitiful thing compared to the shining cities in space we were anticipating sixty years ago. Nothing that I had confidently predicted in my Valedictorian speech has come to pass.

Not that there haven't been technological and cultural advances. No one in my childhood ever imagined the personal computer, cell phones, or the Internet we now take for granted. No one imagined that smallpox and polio would disappear from the earth or that the human genome would be deciphered. The idea that an African-American would be President of the United States wasn't even a fantasy when I was reading those *Saturday Evening Post* articles on future space colonies. Segregation was the order of the day throughout the southern American States, and the popular image of a black man's role was epitomized by Rochester, Jack Benny's butler on his radio and television show.

In other words, between then and now, the future went in a very different and often unexpected direction, as futures are wont to do.

Though I certainly didn't know it at the time, my grade school Valedictorian speech with its emphasis on the future prefigured work I would be doing seven years later when I left Arizona State University and became a spiritual teacher. I found myself part of the newly emerging New Age movement with its emphasis on prophecies of immanent planetary change. As a consequence, particularly after being a co-director in the early Seventies of the international spiritual and New Age community of the Findhorn Foundation in Scotland, I was often asked to give talks on the future. Well into the Eighties, I was considered a spokesperson for the possibilities of cultural and spiritual transformation.

Then my priorities changed. The future became of less interest to me. Instead, I focused on the individual's spiritual journey and the possibilities of transformation with a person's life rather than within the life of a culture. I felt that if people could change and discover their sacredness, the culture would change in response.

I still feel this. But in recent months, the future has come back into my life as a topic to be addressed. With the growing extent of environmental damage, the possibilities of planetary climate change, the global economic meltdown, and the likelihood that the days of cheap energy to power our civilization may be coming to an end as we deplete our finite resources, an increasing number of people are feeling that the world is changing and not necessarily for the better. The familiar, comfortable world many of us grew up with in the industrialized nations, not to mention the glowing technological future we were told to expect, seems liable to disappear, never to come again. The future seems uncertain, even bleak, and people are afraid. It's that fear they talk to me about. It's in response to that fear that I decided to write this little book.

When you're a spiritual teacher, people often assume you have knowledge and insights not given to the normal man on the street. If, in addition, you can communicate with non-physical beings who live in the subtle realms of the spiritual worlds, this assumption is reinforced. Surely your inner contacts can tell you what lies ahead. Surely you can help others face the future and prepare for whatever is coming.

Well, I am a spiritual teacher and I do communicate with non-physical colleagues. And yes, I do have perspectives about the future based on my work and my communications. I will be sharing them throughout this book. But the future is not linear. It's not like the "road ahead," just waiting for us to reach it but which could be viewed in advance if we could rise high enough over intervening obstacles to see it. It's more complex than that. Nothing is carved in stone. The future is emerging and changing even as we formulate our predictions and prophecies about it. The main advice I've had from the subtle realms is this: "Keep all possibilities open; close no doors to the shape the future may take." That is the theme of this book.

If a person believes that the future is ordained, that it is "written" in some book of time, then such a statement makes little sense and can seem like equivocation. For such a person, either I can turn the page of that book and see what is written for our tomorrows or I can't. But for me, that is not how it works; that is not what the future is.

For me, the future is as much who we are as it is what's ahead of us. The future is not only a phenomenon of time; it's a phenomenon of consciousness, in general humanity's consciousness and specifically our consciousnesses. To face the future is to face ourselves, and that's part of what can make it scary. It's also what makes the future malleable, for as we change, it changes. We are partners and collaborators with the future, not its victims. Or perhaps I should say, if the future turns out to be undesirable, then we are not victims of that future but only of ourselves.

I mentioned that when I began my work as a spiritual teacher in 1965 I became part of the nascent New Age movement which was most certainly future-oriented. But initially that was not my orientation. I was interested in the potential for collaborative and co-creative relationships between us and allies in the spiritual realms. This topic is still of great importance to me as I feel it holds promise for healing and bettering the human condition, and I explore it in my book *Subtle Worlds: An Explorer's Field Notes*.

But though I did not focus upon it in my lectures and classes at the time, I was not indifferent to the idea of a potential, emerging New Age. My invisible colleagues had said at different times that humanity was in a time of significant change, and as a young man filled with all the idealism of youth, I was thrilled to think I might be part of helping such a change to occur. Indeed, it was that kind of idealism that fueled the creative work of the Findhorn Foundation, resulting in a spiritual community with a positive vision for the future.

Further, the times themselves seemed to bear out the reality of transformation. While Dylan was singing that the times, they were a'changing, the civil rights and anti-war movements set in motion a reformation of American society, while the counterculture and the human potential movement, emerging at the same time and buttressed by humanistic and transpersonal psychology, created changes in the world far beyond their beginning places in California. Discoveries in science were giving us a new look at the nature of reality. Likewise, when I returned to the United States from Findhorn in 1973, the Arab oil embargo had so challenged a nation increasingly dependent on foreign oil that it set in motion a search for alternatives and an openness to new perspectives in ecology and sustainability. By the end of the Seventies, it seemed like a New Age really was emerging. Positive change was in the air.

But as with the jet packs and the space colonies of my childhood, a funny thing happened on the way to the New Age. The return of cheap oil following the election of Ronald Reagan in 1980 put all the efforts towards alternative energy sources essentially on hold for nearly three decades. Solar power, wind power, geothermal, and other alternatives simply couldn't compete economically with cheap oil when it came down to how much energy a dollar's worth of investment could produce. And society's priorities changed as well, at least until the towers fell on September 11th, 2001. Then everything changed again.

Now, a little more than eight years later, the effects of choices made over the past fifty years, and perhaps especially over the past ten, have set the stage for even more change than ever before. The effects of climate change alone carry the potential of devastating coastal cities and turning now productive farmlands into deserts. When you couple those changes with the global economic troubles and the seeming near bankruptcy of the United States, environmental degradation, and ongoing resource depletion, then Dylan's song seems more like a horrific understatement than a triumphal proclamation.

There is a hope, of course, that things will get better. Certainly our leaders like to assure us that they will, though President Obama's 2010 budget tacitly suggests that it may be a decade or more before they do. But for many business leaders, scientists, and others, things will never go back to the way they were. Change is upon us and it is here to stay, perhaps in a larger and more permanent way than anyone expected or wanted.

This possibility is what creates fear and despair for many people. It is out of this fear and despair, not out of optimism and vision, that they talk with me and ask my opinion on the future. They want to know what is coming and how to face it. I know they want reassurance, but I have none to give, at least not of the kind they'd like to hear. I cannot tell them that change will somehow reverse itself, that life will go back to the "normal" on which their habits are based and maybe even to the point where we really can look forward to robots, jet packs, and colonies on other planets once again.

I cannot say exactly what is coming. The future is fluid. But in spite of the future seeming more bleak and unpromising than it has before in my lifetime—at least according to some of the prognostications—I do feel optimistic. I continue to have a positive vision. I do not feel we are at the end of civilization but at a turning point in what civilization means and in knowing how to build a world that can be a blessing for all.

Why this is so is the subject of this book. I know beyond any question that our greatest enemy is not the image of a bleak future but fear and the constriction of imagination, creativity, and possibility that fear can bring. While I may not know exactly what form the future will take—who does given the dance and flux of possibilities and probabilities in human affairs—I do know that we need not fear. Within ourselves and in our relationships with each other we have the means to be resilient and to shape a future we can live with and even prosper in. Besides, change can mean a chance to grow in new ways. We are in trouble because we have acted out of bad habits as much as out of any evil or malicious design; change gives us a chance to liberate ourselves from those habits and approach the world and each other in new ways. Change can mean promise and gain as much as despair and loss. We should not limit our thinking or our imaginations. As my inner colleagues say, "In a time of change, keep all possibilities open."

Chapter Two
The Apocalyptic Imagination

I forget what year it was, except that it was in the late Sixties before I went to Findhorn. It doesn't matter. In those days, prophecies were a dime and dozen, and every year someone predicted that that was the year civilization as we knew it was going to end. The means varied—nuclear war, earth changes, shifts of consciousness—but the end result was always the same: billions dead but a few thousands who were "ready for a New Age" would survive and build the new civilization.

I generally paid no attention to such prophecies, and my inner contacts were equally dismissive. Their point of view was that if we wanted a new age or a new civilization, we were going to have to create it ourselves, largely by changing our behavior. But this was too slow or too chancy for some who preferred to have transformation served up to us on a large (but usually destructive) platter.

In this particular case, though, the person making the prophecy was an acquaintance, a woman whom I had met a few times on the lecture circuit when we would both be speakers at some New Age or spiritual conference. She was probably twenty years older than I—in those days, being in my very early Twenties, all the speakers and audiences I met in my travels were older than I—and different from the usual New Age prophet or psychic. Before she had developed psychic abilities, she had been a successful businesswoman and had some scientific background which appealed to my own training in that area. We had had good conversations at these conferences, and while I couldn't go along with her prophecies, I respected her as a person.

Her vision was the standard-brand apocalyptic message so common in the New Age movement in those years. Massive earthquakes, tsunamis, volcanic eruptions, tornadoes, and other natural disasters were going to occur on a specific day that year, wiping out most of the major cities, killing millions, if not billions, of people, and blanketing the globe with clouds of debris that block the rays of the sun and initiate a new ice age. Only those who had attuned themselves to the right "vibrational levels of consciousness" would survive by being "spacelifted" by friendly extraterrestrials in flying saucers to their motherships waiting on the dark side of the moon where human astronomers could not see them; it was a technological version of the Rapture expected by many fundamentalist Christians. Then when the atmosphere had cleared and the earth began to warm again, these survivors would be brought back to the planet to begin building the new utopian civilization with the help of the friendly "space brothers."

Put so baldly, it's surprising that anyone would go along with such a prophecy, but she presented it with charm and charisma and had attracted a fairly large following of several thousand people around the world through her newsletters and publications. Besides, back in the Sixties believing in such prophecies was a bit like joining a moveable party going from night club to night club; when one prophecy failed, as it inevitably would, a new one would be announced and rather than wallowing in disappointment and angst, all the true believers would transfer their allegiance to the new one. Simply put, these people were apocalypse junkies.

I could see this—living in California and working in the New Age movement, one could hardly miss it—but I never thought very deeply about why this was so. It just seemed like part of the transformational fever of the times, a fringe manifestation of the same impulse that in different circles was finding expression in the anti-war movement, the civil rights movement, and the counterculture. As I said in the last chapter, change was in the air, and for some people, that change came with a civilization-busting disaster.

Of course, like the others, this woman's prophecy did not come true either. The designated day and hour passed in peace and calm, at least as far as earth changes went. By coincidence, I happened to driving from Los Angeles to San Francisco the day after and passed through the town where she lived. On a whim, I stopped and called her from a pay phone. She had invested years of her life and a great deal of money in spreading the word of her prophetic vision, and I was frankly curious how she was doing. Happy to hear from me, she invited me to her apartment for tea.

Her apartment was beautiful. She had an artist's sensibility and a talent for interior decoration. However, she was a wreck. I no sooner came in the door than she began ranting and spitting with rage, pacing the floor, denouncing her invisible contacts whom she felt had betrayed her by giving her wrong information or by not making the earthquakes happen and the volcanoes erupt. She began to wail, crying over and over again, "I hate this world! I hate this world! It was supposed to be destroyed! I want it destroyed! I can't live in this world!" The venom she was releasing made for a pretty uncomfortable energy in the room.

Nothing I could say would calm her down, so finally I excused myself and gratefully slipped away. After the failure of this prophecy, she dropped out of sight and our paths never crossed again.

Up until then I had assumed that most if not all of these psychically-received and inaccurate prophecies were the result of people tuning in to misinformed or mischievous sources, which certainly exist in the subtle worlds, or to thought-forms and imaginations of fear existing in the collective unconscious of humanity. The latter was certainly a possibility, and I had had experiences of tuning in to such a phenomenon myself. Once in meditation I had had a vision of Soviet tanks and troops crossing into Germany, precipitating World War III. It seemed very real, and I wondered if I were having some precognitive warning. However, in thinking about this and discussing it with my invisible colleagues in the subtle worlds, I realized that this was not a true precognition but a perception of a fearful image that was present in the minds of many people in Europe and the United States as America and the Soviet Union were at a particularly tense moment in their decades-long Cold War dance. Still, at the time, it had appeared convincing. I could see how someone not well versed in the phenomena of the subtle worlds might take such a vision as a genuine prophecy.

After my experience with this woman, though, I began to think that other dynamics were at work promoting these prophecies besides simple psychic error or malfeasance. I knew that there had been other "New Age" movements in the past. Western history has many examples of people prophesying the imminent arrival of the Second Coming of Christ and the subsequent transformation of society. From such prophecies, several movements had arisen attempting to change the status quo. Ultimately all had failed, but some of the statements made by their followers and leaders could, if translated into modern idiom, have appeared in any New Age publication of the Sixties and seemed perfectly appropriate.

Investigating these movements, I soon came to realize that nearly every one of them had been accompanied by apocalyptic prophecies of disasters that would destroy the existing civilization so that a new one could be born. (Two books that chronicle this are *Disaster and the Millennium* by Michael Barkun published in 1974 by Yale University and *The Pursuit of the Millennium* by Norman Cohn, published by Oxford University Press in 1970.) It's not hard to see why. All of these movements began and found their greatest following in the lower classes of society, largely among the poor and the dispossessed. Those who were at the top, mainly the clergy and the nobility, saw no reason for things to change. They like the society as it was. They had the power. But for those without that power, it seemed inconceivable that they could do anything to change the situation without help from an outside force more powerful than their rulers. That force was either God and his angels or the forces of nature. Nowadays, it might be flying saucers and extraterrestrials or the forces of nature.

In other words, from this perspective, it takes a disaster to shatter the entrenched power of the status quo and open the way for a new civilization to take its place. Mere human beings do not have the power to do so.

The world *apocalypse* actually means *revelation* in its Greek roots, but perhaps because of the influence of St. John's Book of Revelation in the Bible with its graphic descriptions of various disasters befalling the world, it has come to mean catastrophe in popular usage. As the meaning has changed, so has an apocalyptic imagination developed in Western culture, often fueled by expectations of the Second Coming of Christ and the consequent end of history as we know it.

I have run into this apocalyptic imagination many times in the past fifty years since I first encountered the idea of a New Age. It was common in the Sixties and Seventies and at least until 1967 was one of the forces that shaped the New Age movement. It died out in the Eighties; everyone was having too good a time to want things to change. But it reared its head again briefly in the run-up to the new millennium, particularly with the Y2K scare. In fact one person I knew, contemplating the projected catastrophic effects that that computer glitch was supposed to cause, said to me, "At last we can begin talking about the end of civilization again!" He had apparently missed his fix of apocalyptic expectation during the previous twenty years. And now it has surfaced again around the prophecies concerning the year 2012.

The apocalyptic imagination isn't just pictures of cities burning beneath mushroom clouds or continents breaking up and sliding into the sea. It's more than a disaster movie we play in our minds as we contemplate the world. The destructive, catastrophic elements are often only a mask covering a deeper complex of attitudes. It's a way of looking at one's self and at life that impacts how a person engages with the present, much less the future.

This attitude combines a sense of elitism with a feeling of powerlessness, hatred with a lack of compassion and perspective, selfishness with conformity, and a desire for revenge with a failure of imagination. It is an attitude that attracts violence the way cow patties attract flies.

When I first encountered the New Age movement in the late Fifties and early Sixties, it was not filled with successful businesspersons or the leaders of society. It was made up of ordinary men and women who saw themselves as the "little guy or gal" in a society of big government, big religion, big institutions. They sincerely desired change for the betterment of humanity but could not imagine themselves creating it; they could only see it coming about as the result of an apocalyptic event.

However, although a person with an apocalyptic vision may feel powerless, this doesn't mean they may not feel special, part of an elite group who "has the truth" and is therefore destined to survive while the rest of humanity either perishes or goes through torments and difficulties from which they will be exempt.

A true, radical transformation of our world, the kind on which a genuinely holistic culture can be based, can't just be for a chosen few. This world belongs to all of us, to all creatures great and small, to all beings physical and non-physical, mortal and spiritual. We are all stakeholders; lasting change will come from efforts on behalf of all. The feeling of elitism, of being better or more special than anyone else, is pernicious, particularly when channeled through the apocalyptic imagination. It cuts the individual off from the rest of humanity and thus further breaks the wholeness of the world, further diminishing the chances of real transformation.

This sense of elitism can be subtle. I have known loving, caring individuals who believed fully in the coming of a New Age following some planetary catastrophe who had no question they would be among those left standing to create the new world. They knew they had the "right vibes." It simply did not occur to them that they might be among those crushed in an earthquake or swept away in a tsunami (any of which were possible as they lived on the coast in California).

Such elitism can breed a lack of compassion. A Baptist minister once confronted me on my way into a hall to give a talk. "Why do you want my wife and children to die," he asked dramatically, surrounded, I realized, by members of his church. "Have you no compassion?" When I asked him what he was talking about, he referred to some of the apocalyptic prophecies going around that spoke of earth changes that would leave millions dead with only New Age believers being spared. I told him that I didn't believe that, but he was on a roll and not to be denied his moment. So I listened to him, thinking that in his own church he preached a form of millennialism that was not all that different from what he was accusing me of, assured that he would be one of the few Raptured into heaven when Christ came again while everyone else either died in the catastrophes that would follow or would suffer in the time of Tribulations. But I knew I would gain nothing from pointing out the hypocrisy of his position. So I excused myself and went into the hall to give my lecture.

In spite of the irony of the pot calling the kettle black, this minister had a point, one that I had spoken about myself at various times. The apocalyptic imagination, whether expressed in Christian, New Age, or some other religious or prophetic terms, is selfish in its setting aside of a select, chosen few and demonstrates a lack of perspective and compassion in its imagination and expectation of the suffering of everyone else.

Further, it often expresses, either overtly or subtly, an underlying feeling of hatred towards the existing culture and often towards humanity itself. My experience with the psychic I described at the beginning of this chapter was an extreme example of this, but unfortunately, while her feelings of loathing for humanity and particularly Western civilization were particularly intense, she was not unique in having them.

This hatred, I have observed, can also reflect anger and a desire for revenge against the culture, perhaps for wrongs that the individual feels he or she has suffered at the hands of the society but perhaps for no other reason than that society hasn't measured up to the person's standards of reality. It is not utopian or perfect enough, and therefore must be destroyed so something better can take its place. Again, this was certainly the attitude of the psychic in my story, but I have encountered it with others as well. It turns a person into an agent of execution rather than an agent of transformation.

These attitudes are bad enough. But the deepest flaw in the apocalyptic vision is the manner in which it constricts the imagination. Can I not imagine other ways to change the future than through destruction and death? If I am feeling powerless and angry at the world around me, perhaps not. This can be particularly true if I've been convinced or have convinced myself that I'm part of a special group, the "chosen few" who by virtue of some element of superiority over the rest of humanity will be part of the new world. But such feelings cut off any search for other, less violent alternatives. They can blind us to other possibilities and potentials within our society, within the world, and most of all within ourselves. Then the real apocalypse becomes the destruction of our creative and compassionate imagination. After all, when you want to change somebody, you don't limit yourself to the assumption that the only way to do so is to kill them.

The apocalyptic imagination can be found worldwide, but it is mostly a phenomenon of Western culture. As such it can both influence and be influenced by another thread that is also found weaving itself through Western history, particularly since the seventeenth century. This is the idea of civilizational decline, the concept that Western culture is flawed and corrupt and either should be destroyed or will inevitably collapse. This idea has become even more pronounced since the rise of industrialism and the growing impact of industrial and technological society upon the natural environment. (If you'd like to investigate the historical roots and expression of this attitude of decline, one place to start is with *The Idea of Decline in Western History*, by Arthur Herman, published by the Free Press in 2007.)

I have certainly run into this assumption of decline and collapse in the fifty years I've been more or less associated with the New Age movement. In fact, I found it usually taken for granted that Western culture was innately evil and life-destroying; its demise would be a favor to the world. I found people all too ready to point out the flaws in Western civilization and industrial society but loathe to find anything to honor or admire. This sense of the corruption of society and the necessity, if not the inevitability, of its decline and collapse played nicely into the feelings of hatred that went along with the apocalyptic imagination.

I bring all this up because Western civilization, indeed *all* civilization, is facing a series of severe planetary challenges. If we are to meet this challenge, we cannot do so seeing the world through apocalyptic glasses or with an assumption that this civilization needs to collapse. Either or both of these prohibit us from seeing what is good and powerful in the civilizations we have created, the tools and opportunities that are at hand, and the potentials and possibilities that may be present. If we feel the game is already lost, or should be lost because humanity has lost the right to be a player, then we have truly sealed our fate. But in such an instance, we are not really facing the future at all but rather staring into the darkness and depths of our own fears, hatreds, and self-loathing.

I want to be clear here. I believe—and this is the essence of the information that I gain from my contact with the subtle worlds—that our modern civilization cannot continue as it is; radical transformation is necessary. Perhaps that transformation will entail loss and suffering. But we cannot proceed assuming this is so or delighting in its possibility.

So much of the apocalyptic thought I've encountered over the years is really about wanting "them" to get what's coming to them, whether "they" are evil governments, evil scientists, evil bankers, evil corporations, evil technology, or simply evil humanity. It's about punishment and revenge, not about a compassionate transformation and the advancement of our species in harmony with the world. And it's often grounded in a fear and cynicism that we're not capable of such advancement, that we are far too flawed as a species to deserve anything other than destruction.

I reject that fear. I believe we are capable. But it will be hard work. My spiritual mentor and friend, a non-physical being I called "John," used to say, "Apocalypse is easy. Death is the easy way out. If you want a new world, you must live your transformation and daily make the choices that will shape the future you want."

The apocalyptic imagination denies the capabilities and potentials that exist in us. It is a failed imagination but a powerful one nonetheless. As we face the future, we need to be aware of its temptations and the way it can distort the challenges we face into reasons to lose hope. When it comes to being able to think creatively, productively, and honestly about the future, the apocalyptic imagination is the equivalent of having a lobotomy.

Chapter Three
Visions of Utopia

When I was fourteen years old, my father got a job as a consultant to a start-up company in Phoenix, Arizona. At the time, we were living in Old Deerfield, Massachusetts. Because the assignment was for the whole summer, Mom went with him while I was sent on to California to spend the three months with my grandmother and my aunt and uncle and cousins who lived in Monterey. It was an idyllic time exploring the beaches and hills around that coastal town, once the capital of Spanish California from 1777 until it was captured in 1846 during the Mexican-American War.

When my parents came to pick me up, they said they had something exciting to share with me. In Phoenix, they had met people who were interested in psychic contact with the non-physical worlds, and they in turn had introduced my folks to a woman who would go into a trance and in that altered state of consciousness would allow an invisible being to speak through her. She had given my father a "reading" in which this being had spoken to him and told him things about his past and future (nearly all of which ultimately proved correct). This session had been recorded, and Dad had the tape and a tape recorder with him. My parents knew that I had also had experiences of these invisible worlds and of non-physical beings all my life and thought I would be interested.

I was *very* interested. I had never met anyone else who had the kind of experiences and contacts that I had had. I had never heard of trance channeling before, having no acquaintance with spiritualism or anything like it, but I had no trouble accepting the possibility that this was a real contact. I listened to this tape two or three times—it was less than an hour in length—and on it I heard this being tell my father of the coming of profound changes that would transform humanity and the earth.

Listening to this tape was my introduction to the concept of the New Age. It was an idea that struck a deep chord within me. I knew that I was hearing something that was important to my life, though I had no idea then that six years later I would become a lecturer and teacher who eventually would be seen as a spokesperson for the New Age movement. Sitting on the floor in my grandmother's living room on that California summer day, listening to this psychic's voice speak to my father about the New Age, I touched unknowingly the path of my own future, one that has shaped my life right to the present moment.

In the last chapter I wrote about the mounting evidence that human civilization is in trouble in a variety of ways, largely of its own making. I used the metaphor that it is falling off the trampoline of progress on which it has been bouncing for the past hundred and fifty years. But is this fall inevitable? Or perhaps I should ask, if it is falling, is it inevitable that we will land hard, crippling ourselves in the process? Are there no positive images of the future that suggest otherwise? Can we not land with grace and style?

One way to explore this is to look briefly at the history of the modern New Age movement and at the concept of the New Age itself. I believe this concept has been misunderstood, for it appears on the surface as an image of the future, and that is how most people have treated it, at least until it turned into a marketing brand and lifestyle choice. But in reality it's an idea about ourselves and our capacity to shape the future in positive ways.

Dad's summer job turned into a permanent one, and we moved to Phoenix in December of 1959. There we became involved with the wild and wooly metaphysical and New Age subculture emerging in Arizona and Southern California. Although the woman who channeled for Dad and produced the tape I heard was not particularly apocalyptic, this was not true for a great many others who were making psychic predictions in the late Fifties and early

Sixties. The modern New Age movement grew out of fairly lurid prophecies foretelling death, destruction and the end of civilization due either to natural disasters or a thermonuclear war. But a strange thing happened on the way to the apocalypse. In the cauldron of the Sixties, the idea of the New Age collided with larger forces of social and cultural change that were agitating and transforming the United States. In the process, it morphed into something else, something that for a time at least was far more powerful and creative than the images from which it emerged.

I was living on the San Francisco Peninsula in the mid-sixties teaching classes on spirituality. It was a time and place of great cultural ferment, challenge and creativity. New insights and approaches to the personality and human development were arising based on the pioneering work of Carl Rogers, Abraham Maslow, and Fritz Pearls along with Stanislof Grof and Roberto Assagioli. Their work gave birth first to humanistic psychology and later in the decade to transpersonal psychology. One of the epicenters for this development was around Stanford University in Palo Alto, not far from where I was living. In fact, one of my students at the time was a man who was one of the very first corporate encounter group trainers using the techniques developed by Carl Rogers. One of the key concepts of these approaches was that we need to take responsibility for the world we experience, an idea simplified by the counterculture to "we create our own reality."

And speaking of the counterculture, during this same time In San Francisco to the north, it was just getting off the ground with extensive experimentation with psychoactive drugs like LSD. The first hippies were beginning to appear in the Height-Ashbury district of the city, leading in 1967 to the Summer of Love in which thousands of people converged from all over the world on Golden Gate Park to celebrate the birth of a "new consciousness." As the song put it, it was the dawning of the Age of Aquarius, for many years the New Age's alter ego. At the same time eastward across the San Francisco Bay at the University of California at Berkeley, students were picketing and boycotting as part of the anti-war movement and on behalf of civil rights.

It was as if the Bay itself was the corpus callosum between the two halves of a great social brain, the left hemisphere of which was in Berkeley while the right hemisphere was in San Francisco. The latter said that a new world would arise from changing our consciousness while the former said change would come when we turned our consciousness to making it happen.

The one characteristic that all these movements and developments had in common was empowerment, a sense that individual people could take charge and change both their lives and the world around them. Social transformation didn't have to depend on some outside agency to destroy the existing culture so a new one could be born. Average people, working together, could make it happen. And they did make it happen, changing the course of the Vietnam War and breaking the hold of segregation in the southern States of America

It was a vital, exciting, creative time. The message of empowerment and of the capacity to effect personal and collective change proved irresistible to the New Age movement, changing it from one of waiting for an apocalypse to one open both to new visions of human and social possibility and to claiming the power to bring those visions into being.

During the late Sixties and throughout most of the Seventies, the New Age movement was largely one of cultural transformation, promoting ecological and environmental sustainability, the development of alternative sources of energy, the emergence of new forms of economics and politics, and the development of human capacities and potentials. It made popular the idea of a "paradigm shift," the emergence of new insights into reality based at first on the discoveries of quantum physics but later on new knowledge coming from the biological sciences, as well as the emergence of whole new disciplines such as the sciences of complexity, chaos and systems theory. It was without question a movement promoting a positive and creative vision of the future, one that humanity could bring into being through its own will and efforts. It might be a challenging transition, but it would not be apocalyptic. It required no destruction, no outside intervention from God, angels, space beings, or natural disasters.

The times were ripe for new visions and new approaches. The

OPEC oil embargo of 1973 with the resulting gasoline shortages and long lines at the gasoline stations convinced many Americans that changes were needed; there was a growing awareness of the negative effects of pollution, not to mention the desire to end both the Vietnam War and the social injustices of racism and segregation. People were willing to experiment and try new things; they were willing to think new thoughts. They saw the future as other than just a continuation of business as usual. The New Age movement in the Seventies provided them with an arena in which this experimentation and exploration could take place. It was a place to flex one's creative imagination in envisioning the future. It supported the courage to take innovative actions.

In 1970, I went to Scotland where I visited the New Age spiritual community of Findhorn. To my surprise, my reputation as a spiritual teacher had preceded me and I was invited to become a co-director of the community. I accepted and spent three years there, becoming a spokesperson for the view of the New Age as an idea of cultural transformation rather than one of apocalypse. When I returned to the United States in 1973, I continued in this role becoming even more identified with the New Age as a positive vision of the future. This put me in the thick of much of the transformative activity of those years, and I was privileged to know many of the men and women who were innovators and pioneers in finding creative ways to change society for the better.

It appeared for a time that genuinely deep and lasting change might take hold in the United States, particularly in the area of environmental conservation and ecological awareness. A reporter for *Newsweek* who was interviewing me as the Seventies turned into the Eighties told me that from her research and perspective, New Age ideas were now the mainstream of American thinking. This was a heady thought; it seemed that a cultural transformation was truly at hand, one wrought not by destruction but by creativity and goodwill and the strength of a positive vision.

Then in the early Eighties, the whole character of the New Age movement changed, and the vision morphed yet again, this time from cultural change to personal development.

The New Age movement was partly a victim of the return of cheap oil, which took away a lot of the pressure that people felt to find energy alternatives and to change their habits of petroleum consumption. From President Carter's diagnosis of a national "malaise" to President Reagan's proclamation of "morning in America," it became all right to feel confident and good about the status quo again. After a time of sacrifice, it was time to pamper ourselves again. The urgency of change simply couldn't stand before the invitation to feel all right about ourselves as a culture. This led to a shift in emphasis in public thinking away from concern for the collective good and toward a focus on individual success and wellbeing.

In the New Age movement this took the form of an increasing emphasis on personal development, psychic phenomena, mystical consciousness, self-esteem, spiritual wellbeing, and self-help techniques; the focus became more introspective. It was during this time that the New Age gained a reputation for being narcissistic, navel-gazing, and unconcerned with the "real world." "New Age" itself came to be defined not as a vision of the future, calling for individual and collective effort, but as a lifestyle. It became simply a brand for certain kinds of food, clothing, music, literature, and spirituality. And as this happened, I became less and less associated with the New Age until today I have hardly any connection to what's left of that movement.

I do not intend here to write a history of the New Age movement. There are some excellent books that cover some of that territory, though I've yet to find a truly comprehensive history of the movement. If you are interested, two excellent books are *Unfinished Evolution* by Teena Booth and *Odyssey of a Practical Visionary* by Dr. Belden Paulson. Suffice it to say that by the mid nineteen-eighties, the whole character of the New Age movement changed. It was no longer apocalyptic, but it wasn't a vision of the future either.

On the other hand, the New Age never really was a specific image of the future anyway. It certainly didn't present images of a possible tomorrow with the same detail that my old *Saturday Evening Post* magazines did. New Age speculations ran more to the qualities that a new culture would have, such as being "ecological" and "holistic." It was to be a time when peace really would "guide the planets" and love "steer the stars," a time of harmony between nations and between humanity and nature. In short, it postulated the coming of utopia, the "Golden Age" of which humanity has dreamt for millennia.

This is not to say that there weren't people thinking seriously and specifically about new kinds of politics, economics, technology, alternative energy sources, ecological sustainability, community organization, non-violent conflict resolution, and the like, and coming up with innovative ideas and designs. But on the whole, the New Age idea was less about such specifics and more about the possibility of transformation itself and the expectation of a better world ahead of us.

The utopian imagination has been as powerful a part of Western civilization, indeed of world history, as the apocalyptic imagination, and at times the two have intertwined — as they did at the beginning of the New Age movement — when the path to a better world is seen as passing through the gateway of disaster. But although both are visions of change, their roots are different. The imagination of apocalypse can arise and be nourished, as I wrote in the last chapter, from darker places within our thoughts and emotions, whereas utopian thought often celebrates the inspiring capacities of the human being to create a positive society.

The challenge is that the expectation of utopia, as much as that of apocalypse, can lead to a diminishment of our capacity to deal with the future. Apocalypse can lead us into fantasies of destruction, but utopia can lead us into fantasies of transformation. This was certainly true within the New Age movement where many people had expectations that a sudden transformation of consciousness, often seen as literally occurring overnight or between one minute and another, would change everything and bring a new world into being. We can see this same expectation in many of the prophecies surrounding the year 2012, the current poster child for both apocalyptic and utopian imaginations.

I will write more fully about the idea of a "planetary shift in consciousness" in a later chapter. The point I wish to make here is simply that the utopian imagination can disempower us not through fear or despair but through an overestimation of human potential or a failure to face the present. The person swayed by apocalypse may hate the present and thus desire its destruction, but the person dazzled by the allure of utopian possibilities may simply not see the present at all. Why bother dealing with the reality of the moment when all is soon to be transformed by forces of Light and benevolence? Or, from a humanist's point of view, why bother if the creative power of humanity is sufficient to meet all challenges and the present will soon become a better future shaped by the unstoppable hand of progress?

The idea of progress, that civilization is moving steadily onward and upward to ever greater heights of accomplishment, has been the most persuasive utopian myth in modern Western history since at least the Eighteenth Century. It assumes that the future cannot help but be brighter and better than the present. The remarkable advancement of science and technology is used as evidence supporting this assumption, and for a large part of the world's population, things are better now than they were fifty or a hundred years ago. This idea has also been bolstered by a popular misunderstanding of Darwin's theory of evolution. Evolution is not a theory of progress of but adaptation. It doesn't predict that organisms will getter better from one generation to the next but only that they will survive through adapting to changing environmental conditions.

But this distinction was lost when the idea of evolution was applied to human culture. Progress, particularly in science and technology, was seen as a measure of evolution. Western society was seen as the most evolved civilization on earth, and according to the utopian myth of progress, it would continue to get better and better and more and more powerful. This was the image of the future unabashedly presented to me as a child by magazines like the *Saturday Evening Post*. It was taken for granted, as I said, that there would be colonies on the moon and on Mars by the time I was an adult, and it was also taken for granted (at least until Sputnik was launched) that those colonies would be American.

Part of what enabled the New Age movement to move from the fringe of society into the mainstream as much as it did was the fact that once it shed its apocalyptic focus, it became identified as an evolutionary movement and thus fully in tune with the dominant myth of progress. The New Age might proclaim the transformation of society, but this transformation was seen as a continuation of human progress and the evolution of consciousness and society.

The irony with the idea of progress is that it is not necessarily as future-oriented as it seems on the surface; it is often more a statement of the present and the desire to keep things as they are, only better, than it is a vision of a possible alternative future.

Back in 1973 when I had just returned from Findhorn and found myself being asked to give lectures on the New Age, its meaning and its possibilities, I had the delight and privilege of meeting Elise Boulding, a sociologist and a Quaker, and a very respected and influential scholar and activist for peace. She had translated into English a book by a Dutch futurist, Dr. Fred Polak, which had just been published. It was called *The Image of the Future*, and she felt what he had to say was germane to my own work. I immediately purchased a copy and found that she was very right.

Here is an excerpt from the Foreword, written by her husband, the economist Kenneth Boulding:

> *The human condition can almost be summed up in the observation that, whereas all experiences are of the past, all decisions are about the future. It is the great task of human knowledge to bridge this gap and to find those patterns in the past which can be projected into the future as realistic images. The image of the future, therefore, is the key to all choice-oriented behavior. The general character and quality of the images of the future which prevail in a society is therefore the most important due to its overall dynamics. The individual's image of the future is likewise the most significant determinant of his personal behavior.*

Polak's book is an examination of the relationship between

different images of the future and the historical cultures that held them. The question he asks is, "What is the impact of an image of the future on a society." The answer, as previewed in Boulding's remarks, is that this image affects the behavior and choices of that society. But he noted an important difference between what he called a true image of the future and merely an image of progress, even though on the surface the two might seem the same. An image of progress is simply a continuation of the status quo though in a bigger and better or more advanced state. It does not challenge the existing society in any truly creative or transformative way. An image of the future, on the other hand, presents the future as other, as that which is radically different and which challenges the assumptions of the current society.

Here's an example. A future in which the automobile becomes more technologically sophisticated and efficient, even one in which it is powered by something other than gasoline, is an image of progress. It does not change the underlying assumption that we need to have automobiles as transportation. An image of the future, on the other hand, would challenge that assumption and invite the society to think of wholly different ways of meeting its transportation needs.

In my lectures of that time, I often used the television show *Star Trek* as another example of the difference between an image of progress and an image of the future. *Star Trek* was a science fiction drama in which the action took place several hundred years in the future in a Federation (headed, naturally, by human beings from earth) in which starships explored the galaxy with crews made up of members of different alien species all working cooperatively together. This was a future one could aspire towards, and over the years, I have met a number of engineers and scientists who were inspired by the positive vision of the future that *Star Trek* presented. However, it did not take a very close analysis to see that the Federation was in effect twentieth-century America and the challenges that the show dealt with were basically Twentieth-century problems.

Because *Star Trek* was a popular entertainment, it could hardly be otherwise. A true depiction of what a galaxy-spanning, multi-species culture might be like would probably be nothing anyone at the moment could imagine. *Star Trek* represented American society that had progressed to the stars while remaining familiar and understandable to present-day Americans.

In his historical analysis, Polak discovered something interesting. He found that while a culture had a true image of the future, an image that challenged the status quo, it advanced significantly in all its creative endeavors. When, however, this image of the future was replaced with an image of progress, that culture began to decline and eventually became stagnant or disappeared. Looking at late Twentieth-Century Western Civilization, Polak concluded that we had lost our image of the future and had substituted an image of progress in its place.

This is what happened to the New Age movement as well. In the Seventies at its most creative, it was an exploration of images of the future and of human potential that challenged all of us to think in new ways, outside the box, of what a new and transformed society might be and how it might be brought into being. In the Eighties and beyond, however, it turned into an image of progress—and an image of purely personal progress at that—as it became a self-help movement focused on giving us better bodies, better personalities, and better consciousnesses but not necessarily transformed ones.

The idea of progress as inevitable and always beneficial is part of the utopian imagination. As such it presents us not with a clear vision of either the present or of possibilities but entices us with mind-candy. It presents a future it would like, but it does not necessarily see the future that could be or that needs to be. It sees the future as evolution, but in the process forgets that evolution does not mean *better* but *more adapted*. The most positive future for a society may not be the one that looks the best or seems the most progressive, but the one that is most adapted to and harmonious with its world and in the process most in touch with its own wholeness and creativity as well.

Chapter Four
Falling from the Trampoline

When I was in high school, we had a gymnastics team. The captain was a handsome, popular fellow who seemed like one of those golden people before whom life bows and offers its greatest treasures. I didn't know him, for I was a lowly freshman and he a god-like senior, but he was well-known and well-liked around the campus. Then one day disaster struck. While working out on a trampoline, he made an error and landed wrong, breaking his spine. In one horrific moment he went from a young athlete to a quadriplegic, paralyzed from the neck down.

This accident affected me deeply. For one thing it gave me a lasting distrust of trampolines. But in a more important way, it introduced me to tragedy, something that had been absent from my young life. I can still remember fifty years later the hollow, aching feeling I had in the pit of my stomach when I learned of the accident. All I could think of was how his future had been taken from him. I could feel the abrupt transition from being young, healthy and having a rich future ahead of him to being confined to a bed, unable to move for however many years he might live. The horror of it filled my imagination for days afterward. It made me realize how fragile the future could be and how quickly and unexpectedly things could change.

Nothing hurts us in quite the same way as a future denied. Expecting that things will go in a certain way and then suddenly discovering that they won't can be profoundly disorienting. It's as if the world we knew suddenly ceased to exist. Grief, anger, denial, and despair are only some of the emotions that can arise as a result.

From many indications, this is the state that modern civilization finds itself in. It's as if we have been in the air, bouncing on the trampoline of progress, soaring ever higher, and then we realize we have made a mistake. We have flipped wrong or twisted badly. Now we're about to fall and break our necks, and as a result, the future we had imagined for ourselves will no longer come to pass. Instead, something far more constricting, far more limited, and even far more deadly lies ahead.

For an increasing number of people, this is no metaphor. This is exactly what is happening or about to happen. This prospect of the collapse of modern technological civilization, can be a source of fear, despair, denial, or, if a person is caught up in an apocalyptic imagination, even a source of secret (or not so secret) delight. Conversely, if I am bedazzled by a utopian imagination, particularly that of the idea of inevitable progress, I can ignore that anything untoward is happening at all. I can be so entranced by the possibilities ahead that I fail to see what is really happening in the present. I become disassociated from current reality.

Is our civilization really falling off the trampoline?

Obviously there are those who will say no or who at most will say, "Yes, but we'll only sprain an ankle. That will slow us down for awhile, but no big deal. We'll be up and fine in no time." The idea of a positive future is hard to give up, and as we'll see in later chapters, it's not necessarily right to do so, certainly not in any absolute way.

We all want a positive, happy, abundant future. But we need to confront the nature of our current reality if we are to truly face the future in any creative and intelligent way. There is mounting evidence from many sources that at the very least, we're in for a difficult ride in the Twenty-First century, and at the worst…well, it should satisfy the most jaded aficionado of apocalyptic scenarios.

In the middle Fifties, when I was a child living on an American air base in Morocco, a geoscientist named M. King Hubbert working for Shell Oil, developed a theory that the rate of oil production for any oil field would over time resemble a bell curve. The peak of that curve was the time when the maximum rate of extraction would occur, after which production would decline. He presented his theory in a paper in 1956 to the American Petroleum Institute and used it to accurately predict when the United States would reach peak oil production in the 1970s. Subsequently, his mathematical model has been used to predict when global peak oil production will take place; depending on the variables used in the model, this has either already occurred or will occur within the next decade.

The concept of peak oil doesn't mean that suddenly at that point there is no more oil to be had. Peak oil represents the moment of maximum production which itself is a product of both resource availability and the ease and cost of extracting it. Following this peak, oil (or any other resource, for the model is not confined just to petroleum) is still available but in a form that is increasingly more difficult or more expensive to extract. In effect the peak oil model predicts when cheap oil begins to become less and less available.

Underlying the concept of peak oil is a very simple fact. We live on a finite world with finite resources. You can only use such resources for so long before they're gone. If a farmer gave me sixty eggs but no chickens when he moved away and I eat an egg for breakfast every morning, there will come a day two months from now when I'll have to eat oatmeal instead. The eggs will be gone, and without chickens I'll have no way to replace them.

In the case of petroleum, the chickens have long since disappeared. When I drive my car, I am burning up highly concentrated solar energy that at one time was part of the bodies of ancient plants and animals. These plants and animals were the chickens of the petroleum egg, and it took millions of years of unremitting heat and pressure in the bowls of the earth to turn the carbon compounds of their dead bodies into oil. There is no infinite supply. We have been using it for the past hundred years as if there were no tomorrow. But there is always a tomorrow, and peak oil says that it will contain less and less petroleum costing more and more dollars.

"Well," a person might say, "so I'll just pay a bit more at the gasoline pump over the next few years. Big deal. I'll get an electric car." But gasoline is not the only petroleum product. Plastics come from oil, as do fertilizers, many medicines, polyester clothing, waxes and lubricants of various kinds, crayons, house paint, eyeglasses, enamel, cameras, cell phones, I-pods... the list goes on and on, covering over six thousand common items that are used daily. It isn't just gasoline that will cost more; it's everything else as well, including other forms of energy.

For a civilization that is built on the availability of cheap energy, the implications of such rising costs can be staggering. We already have seen in the United States in recent years the negative impact that just a slight rise in gasoline prices can have on the economy as a whole. Imagine such price increases across the board for not only gasoline but food, manufacturing goods of all kinds, electricity and natural gas, medicines, health care. There will come a point when the economy cannot take it and will break or will fracture into a class of the very rich and a class of everyone else living roughly like medieval serfs because we can't afford anything else.

But it's not just the economy. Most of the technology that keeps our civilization going runs on cheap energy. Take away that energy, either because the resources just aren't available or they've become too expensive, and what happens? For instance, the server farms that power the Internet require huge expenditures of energy. What happens when that energy simply isn't available or costs too much? What happens to the Internet if the servers cannot function, or at best only function for periods of the day when rationed electricity becomes available? We can see examples of the possibilities because similar conditions exist in third world countries today. The implication of peak oil is that the United States and other industrialized nations constituting what is now called the First World or the Developed World will end up in the foreseeable future with the standard of living equivalent to what these third and fourth world countries have now.

This is not the future than most Americans are expecting. It's the equivalent of having the energy spine of our civilization snapped, leaving us paralyzed and constricted compared to what we can do today. Are we in any way prepared mentally, emotionally, or spiritually, not to mention physically and socially, for such an eventuality?

A good friend of mine is John Michael Greer. I first met him some years ago at a spiritual conference where he and I were both giving presentations, though I had known of him before then as the author of many excellent books on spirituality, Western philosophy and esoterics. John also is the Archdruid of the Ancient Order of Druidry in America, which he says lets him wear funny hats. For some years I only knew him as a fellow spiritual teacher. Then I discovered that ever since the seventies he has been a serious researcher and student of alternative energy, environmental sustainability, and ecology. It turned out that he was one of the leading thinkers and writers about peak oil and its possible consequences, sharing his insights in his Internet blog, *The Archdruid Report*.

He is an articulate spokesperson in giving warning of the impact of resource depletion on our economy and technology, indeed on our civilization as a whole. What I like about John's work is that he is not apocalyptic, and he offers positive steps that people can take to deal with a potential reversal of industrial society to third world status. He is not a prophet of hopelessness or one who uses peak oil simply as an excuse to express antipathy or even hatred of industrial or Western civilization. If you wish to explore the future as seen through the lens of peak oil, I recommend both his blog and his two books on the subject, *The Long Descent: A Users Guide to the End of the Industrial Age* and *The Ecotechnic Future: Envisioning a Post-Peak World.*

Another individual writing on peak oil and its effects is Carolyn Baker, a professor of history and a former psychotherapist. I am most familiar with her through her excellent book *Sacred Demise: Walking the Spiritual Path of Industrial Civilization's Collapse* and her website. She is one of the few people writing about the spiritual, moral, and psychological implications of our culture's falling off its trampoline.

John and Carolyn are not doomsayers as much as they are informed observers of the consequences of our society's actions and wastefulness in a world of finite resources. But there are those who are prophesying doom and the imminent arrival of apocalypse. Naturally, there are those who refute such claims. Some of these refutations stem simply, as far as I can tell, from an unwillingness to face a future of civilizational downsizing and represent a form of denial, but others are well-reasoned and backed by statistics and figures. Of course, data and numbers can be massaged and used by the proponents of any point of view to support their position, and a layperson without the time or skills to do the research and ferret out the information for himself or herself can feel challenged to sort out conflicting claims. But if we are to face the future knowledgably and not simply emotionally or fearfully, we need to be open to different points of view because the whole picture is undoubtedly more complex than any one person or perspective can encompass.

For this reason, while respecting John and Carolyn's perspectives, I try to seek out opposite points of view that have a similar standard of clarity and intellectual integrity. One source I've found helpful is a blog called unimaginatively but certainly unambiguously *Peak Oil Debunked*. This title is misleading as the blogger, identifying himself simply as "JD," doesn't debunk the idea of peak oil at all. He mainly takes exception, as would I, with many of the doomsday predictions and the fear-mongering that some in the peak oil community are promoting. In effect, he writes articles drawing on a variety of scientific and scholarly sources to challenge not the concept of peak oil itself but its use by those captivated by the apocalyptic imagination and by a desire to see civilization itself (and particularly Western civilization) come to an end. The articles are of varying quality and objectivity, but on the whole they allow a broader picture to emerge—for me, at least—than if I only paid attention one point of view.

No one denies that we live on a planet with finite resources. It has been estimated that for everyone on earth to live a lifestyle equivalent to that of the average citizen in North America would require the resource capacity of three or four more earths. Unfortunately, God forgot to sprinkle a few extra planets like ours around the solar system. Likewise, no one doubts that we can overshoot those resources, demanding more than there is in order to keep civilization going at its current pace and complexity. There are, however, reasoned and reasonable differences of opinion among those who study this issue as to how this might happen or when peak oil may occur and at what rate the subsequent decline in production and cheap energy may take place. For some, it's a steep decline occurring rapidly and for others it's a gentler slope. Likewise, no one can predict exactly what all the consequences may be, though resource wars (which have already begun in small ways) may be one of them.

Likewise, there are differing opinions on whether or not alternative energy sources can be found to take up the slack and keep things going as oil and other critical resources become less available and more expensive. It's almost in our genetic code in Western culture to assume that if there's a problem, some new technology will take care of it. We are like an audience waiting for the magician to pull a rabbit out of his hat and confident that he will do so.

John Michael Greer believes that in this case the magician's hat will be empty and sees little chance technology will save the day. One reason he feels this way is not due to any lack of respect for human ingenuity or for scientific innovation but because it is highly likely that any new technology of sufficient complexity and power to meet the increasing energy demands of a planet-wide technological culture will itself be dependent for its development and implementation on the very petroleum and other resources that are diminishing. For John, the basic problem of overshooting finite resources is not so much a problem to be solved by some technological fix as a condition to which we now need to adapt.

Stewart Brand, the founder of *Co-Evolution Quarterly* and for decades one of the leading spokespersons of the environmental movement, believes on the other hand that there are some rabbits the magician can pull out. He describes what these might be in his new book, *Whole Earth Discipline: An Ecopragmatist Manifesto*. I will have more to say on this myself in a later chapter.

If resource depletion as exemplified by peak oil were the only problem facing us, it would be challenging enough. But it's not. We are also facing a variety of environmental threats. Many of these are dire, such as the pollution of the oceans and its impact on the food chains that support life, but the most threatening is undoubtedly climate change.

I live a few miles east of Seattle, Washington. Seattle occupies a strip of land between Puget Sound on the west and Lake Washington, the second largest lake in the State of Washington, on the east. On the eastern shore of this lake is Bellevue, the fourth largest city in the State. One day some years ago, I was driving along the freeway just east of Bellevue when suddenly I was startled to see all the land to the west of me underwater. It was as if the Sound had risen, flooding Seattle and pouring water into Lake Washington which had in turn risen and flooded Bellevue. This vision only lasted a few seconds and then disappeared.

Such visions are not really prophecies; they are shadows of possibilities. I know from my inner experiences that they can come from a number of different sources, including projections of fear from the collective unconscious. However, if global climate change proceeds as currently predicted by climatologists and other scientists, we will see a rising of sea levels throughout the world as the whole heats up and polar ice melts. Coastal cities are most definitely at risk. Perhaps I had seen a glimpse of a possible future.

One effect of climate change is to turn food and water into scarce resources. With rising temperatures, desertification will increase, affecting much of the planet's most fertile cropland, reducing the amount of food humanity can produce. Starvation is one consequence, as are mass migrations as people seek to leave the areas that can no longer support them. In fact, as the reporter Stephan Faris describes in his book *Forecast*, such effects of changing climate are already occurring. For instance, parts of North Africa that were arable only a generation ago have now become barren and without water due to persistent draught and warmer temperatures; as a consequence, the local populations have been migrating north into Europe seeking employment, food, shelter and new means of survival. If climate change continues, this movement may be only a trickle compared to what will happen over the next twenty years. European society is already having difficulty absorbing and accepting the current level of immigration. What will happen if it keeps increasing with each passing year?

Peak oil and climate change are more than enough to push us off the trampoline, but they don't exhaust the list of potential problems facing us. As modern civilization has grown technologically, we have gained the ability to do many things that previously were not possible. The Internet, for example, is truly one of the wonders of the world. Its capacity to allow for unprecedented global communication and the pooling and sharing of information and experience can provide a foundation for a true planetary awareness to develop within humanity, a global mind. But our technological development has come at a price. Even without such threats as peak oil or global warming and climate change, the complexity of society makes it vulnerable to breakdowns and to attack.

For instance, it isn't just physical terrorism that threatens us, though a "dirty bomb" released in a major city would ruin a lot of peoples' days for years to come; cyberterrorism poses a more fundamental danger. Already there are hundreds, if not thousands, of attempts daily to hack sensitive computer networks that run key installations such as the electrical power grid in the United States. To combat this threat, the United States has created the U.S. Cyber Command, recognizing that the nation is involved in a wholly new kind of invisible warfare. A successful "cyberstrike" could bring about the collapse of banking, electrical distribution, transportation, air service, or any number of other critical components of a modern technological society.

It's just one more way we can fall off the trampoline.

I haven't even mentioned the economic meltdown that occurred in 2008 and nearly sent the world into a depression. As I write these words in February, 2010, we're not out of the woods yet. The planetary economic system continues to rumble with aftershocks that might yet bring the whole thing crashing down. The problem is compounded not just by the greed of a few in high places but by the political gridlock and partisan warfare that paralyzes the ability of the government to act creatively and effectively on this and many of the other challenges we face. Frankly, there are times when I read the paper or watch the evening news that I feel I'm living in the last days of the Roman Empire when government dissolved into a free-for-all with factions vying for power, corruption was rampant, and no one exhibited a regard for the common good or a commitment to public service.

Peak oil, resource depletion, global climate change, environmental degradation and pollution, economic instability and bankruptcy, political gridlock, terrorism: these are all conditions that are shaping our tomorrows. When we face the future, they are there in front of us in one form or another. We cannot pretend they don't exist. And they are scary. They present a future that inspires dismay and fear.

It is this fear that that prompts people to write to me or talk with me about the future. They assume that because I'm a spiritual teacher who communicates with non-physical beings in the subtle worlds, I will have "inside information," so to speak, about what's ahead of us. After all, aren't the non-physical worlds the source of prophecy in the first place? Who better to know the future than a spiritual being who, most people assume, can see and know everything? And, of course, what goes unsaid (well, most of the time anyway) is the hope that from a higher, spiritual perspective, I will paint a rosier picture, one that will sweep the negative images away and assure people that the experts who promote them are wrong.

This is not surprising in the least. We all want to know that we're going to be all right. We all want safety. We all want the future of our fondest dreams and not of our direst nightmares.

Unfortunately, I don't have that kind of information. In my own experience at least, that's not how the subtle worlds work. They're not like a huge crystal ball in which the future stands revealed for anyone with the ability to see. The future is always unfolding and emerging. Every day it is being shaped by the decisions and choices we make, the actions we take, the beliefs we hold.

But if I cannot offer comforting prophecies, what I *can* suggest are ways to participate in this shaping. There are many fine people, skilled and knowledgeable in their own fields, who are suggesting things we can do in the physical world to make a better future. What I want to suggest are things we can do in cooperation with the invisible worlds to promote the same end. I call this process subtle activism. This may not seem like much in the face of our global challenges, but in fact it puts us in touch with some of the greatest powers in the world: the powers of imagination, of partnership, of love, of creativity...and of miracles.

The first step in tapping those powers is to determine just what we mean by "the future."

Chapter Five
The Three Futures

What is the future?

On the surface, this seems like a nonsensical question. The future is what happens a few minutes, hours, days, and weeks from now. It is what is ahead of us in time. It is the content of our tomorrows.

This assumes that anything is ahead of us, that time is like a road or river stretching like a line ahead of us and along which we move from the past through the present to the future. Certainly this is the picture upon which Western civilization has been based for millennia. It's not the only way that the time or the future can be conceptualized, however. Some civilizations have seen time as a circle rather than a line, endlessly repeating itself with slight variations much as the winter always follows autumn and gives way to spring and summer. And there have been cultures that have no concept of time whatsoever and do quite well without it, living in an endless present.

The nature of time, however, is a discussion that is beyond the scope of this book. Our topic is facing the future, so we will take as a given that the future exists and can be faced. But even saying this, there is more to the experience of the future than just a prediction of what's coming tomorrow.

Recently my wife and I celebrated our twenty-eighth wedding anniversary. Throughout our marriage, we have both been pretty good about remembering this date, but there have been one or two occasions when life was very busy and it snuck up on us, so to speak. At such moments, either Julia or I would forget that our anniversary was upon us, thinking we still had a few days to go. To keep this from happening, I created a computer calendar file that would automatically remind me as the anniversary approached.

When my parents were married, their wedding dinner was in a Chinese restaurant in New York City. Consequently, on their anniversary, they always had a Chinese meal in celebration. Julia and I don't actually have a routine like that, so as the big day approaches, I find myself thinking of various possibilities of things we could do. I think of past anniversaries. I think of our wedding, conducted by a minister friend of ours in his home the day before I was to lead a workshop that he had set up. Mostly, I think of how much I love my wife, of the many good times we've had together, and of my desire that we have many years more, growing old together. In spite of these thoughts and plans, however, more often than not on the morning of our anniversary, we look at each other and ask, "Well, what would you like to do to celebrate?" Depending on circumstances, each year the answer is different.

In this simple story, three different futures are represented. First there is the anniversary itself. It is a date I can inscribe on the calendar, an event to look forward to, a day to remember. And it is an event on the calendar because of actions we took twenty-eight years ago. It is a consequence of our getting married.

I call this the *consequential future*. Certain things will happen tomorrow because of actions or conditions that have happened in the past. The sun will rise tomorrow as a consequence of celestial mechanics that govern the rotation of the earth on its axis as it revolves around the sun. Every four years there will be a Presidential election here in the United States because of legal requirements set forth in the Constitution that gave birth to this country. My parents always had a Chinese meal on their anniversary because that was what they had eaten for dinner the day they were married. This future is made up of consequences of past actions and choices.

Second, as our anniversary approaches, I begin to imagine what it will be like and what we might do. I think of our marriage and all the feelings and memories that surround it. I may even make plans for the big day.

I call this the *imaginal future*. It is the future as I imagine it will be or could be. It is the future as I shape it in my thinking and feeling, the future as represented by plans and hopes. If I carry out my intentions and all goes well as planned, then this will be the future that manifests.

Often this future is one of habit and repetition simply because I can't imagine anything different. I may stay in a dead-end job because I can't imagine myself doing anything different or taking the risk of trying something new. I may stay in a bad relationship for the same reason. Then my future is shaped by my habits and my fears. I can't see past the images I know. I surrender my future to the tyranny of the familiar.

The third future is what happens when my wife and I look at each other and say, "What shall we do today?" We are open to possibility. The future is undetermined. It lives in our creativity in the moment. We are its shapers, and until we make a choice, it has no shape.

I call this the *creative future*. In a way, it's not really a future at all in the sense of something existing in time. Instead, it's the future as it lives in the womb of my creativity. It is an attitude towards the future, an attitude open to possibility and potential. More precisely, it's an attitude towards time itself, one that refuses to be limited in thinking or feeling—or if possible, in action--either by the past or by the future but honors the power of the present to unfold and shape what is. It's a state of consciousness that says, "In this moment I can choose and shape what has never happened before. In this moment I am free."

When Julia and I look at each other and say, "What shall we choose to do today to celebrate," we don't have any specific image in mind. We are not imagining anything. We are acknowledging our power to imagine a future. In that moment, all possibilities lie open before us. The future of our anniversary lies in us waiting to be created.

Of course, there are limits. We might choose to go to Paris to celebrate or to climb Mt. Rainier. Either would be great, but neither is likely. Our bank account won't support the one, and my lungs won't support the other. Neither possibility, strictly speaking is impossible, though. A friend might call up and say, "By the way, I have two tickets to Paris; would you like to go?" Stranger things have happened in our lives. And given oxygen bottles and a team of people to help me (i.e. carry me), I probably could make it to the summit of Mt. Rainier. But the fact that something is theoretically possible doesn't mean it's probable. We won't spend our anniversary waiting around for either to happen.

The fact that there are limits, though, doesn't negate or lessen the power of this creative future. Boundaries upon what is possible don't make me less creative; they only focus and determine the direction in which that creativity will express itself. To say that I can't be creative simply because I have limitations in either my wallet or my body is to deny the wonder and power of my innate capacity to bring something new into being.

These three futures overlap and blend with each other. The creative future leads to an imaginal future based on my choices and the plans I form out of my imagination become events that lead to consequences as I take action. It can work in the other direction, too. The existence of consequences can shape my imagination and, as I said, focus the direction of my creativity.

When the gymnastics team captain at my high school broke his back, the consequences were severe. His life became very constrained compared to what it had been before the accident. And I do not know what happened to him afterward. But there have certainly been examples of quadriplegics who have continued to accomplish things and lead creative lives, Christopher Reeves, the actor, being a prime example. There were choices he could no longer make and things he could no longer do, but by the same token, there were new choices and new actions he could take that inspired the world and greatly helped the cause of others who were paralyzed as he was. The issue is not how we're limited but what we do within those limitations.

If the scenarios of peak oil are true, then this is what our civilization may be facing. We will face constraints upon what we can do imposed by the loss of cheap oil and the energy it provides. But that doesn't mean we lose the capacity to create a different kind of culture with a different technology.

When it comes to the future, the consequential future can never take away the creative future or the power of our imagination.

When people ask me about the future and what it will bring or express fear and dismay over various predictions, what troubles them is not the creative future. They are not afraid of being creative; in fact, they are probably not even thinking of being creative; fear has a way of constricting our creativity and our sense of possibility. The problem with the future is really the problem of consequences and usually unintended ones at that. It's the consequential future that troubles us.

Here we have a problem that many doctors are all too familiar with. Some years ago I had a viral infection in my heart that caused congestive heart failure. It sounds serious, and potentially it is, but at the time at least it was not life-threatening. One of the valves of my heart doesn't work as efficiently as it did before the infection, and as a consequence, fluid can back up into my lungs. The treatment is to make sure I don't retain water in my body, and that means I have to watch my salt intake. I'm someone who loves salty food, but now for my continued health, I have to adjust to a very low sodium diet or even no sodium.

This has not been easy. I'd like to have the lifestyle I had before the infection with no worry about eating salty food, but I can't. Those days are over. I needed to change my diet. I could see this as a limitation upon me and that I'm being denied the foods I liked to eat, or I could see it as a creative challenge and an opportunity to explore new ways of cooking and eating.

I've chosen the latter course as the alternatives are not pleasant—I have no desire for a heart attack or cardiac asthma—and in the process I've discovered whole new food possibilities. And I've discovered as well that by cutting way down on the salt I use, I can taste foods in ways I never used to. I don't have the potato chip future I thought I'd have when I was younger and healthier, but I like the future that's newly unfolding.

In adapting, I need to adjust my imaginal future. I have had to imagine meals and cooking in new and different ways, and I've had to imagine different ways of shopping as well (most everything in the average grocery store—and even in many health food stores—has an overabundance of sodium in it). It's been work making the change, but it's been exciting, too, and I feel better. I've been able to blend my consequential future—the product of the heart infection and its consequences—with my creative future to bring something new into being in my life.

It's important to remember that a consequential future is not necessarily set in stone. The sequence of cause and effect may give a particular set of consequences momentum and a high probability, but that doesn't mean those consequences are one hundred percent certain. For instance, my cardiologist told me that my heart could heal itself, returning me to normal (though probably not if I put pressure on it through continuing a salty diet).

When we read about the potential effects of global warming—the rise of sea levels, flooding coastal cities, or the desertification of farm lands, reducing the food supply and causing widespread starvation—we are looking at the consequential future. All these effects are the consequences of something else. These consequences can be frightening, and they should be, if we are to change. Contemplating a heart attack is not a particularly uplifting image for my future, either.

But we can become too fixated on consequences. I don't live my life in fear of my heart failing. I seek creative ways to reorder my life so I can enjoy health and a lifestyle I can enjoy. One major element of this is realizing that joy in one's life comes from within and not from outer conditions alone. It's a choice I can make as part of my creative future rather than waiting for life to bring me joy and feeling down when it doesn't. Similarly, I don't wake up each morning thinking "Well, this is one day closer to the collapse of industrial civilization." I wake up thinking, "What a wonderful day! What a privilege to have another day here on earth. What can I do today to help the world be a better place than it was yesterday?"

Of course the future is something that happens outside of me. If an earthquake strikes the Puget Sound area where I live, it won't be as pleasant a day as if it doesn't (and the earth scientists tell us that we're overdue for a good shaking here in this area, as we are on a major fault line). But the future is not just something unfolding around me. It is also what is unfolding within me. You and I, we are the future as much as consequential events are the future as well.

As a spiritual teacher, I see this relationship between the consequential and the creative future (with the imaginal future in-between) through a particular lens. For instance, take the idea of karma. In the popular conception of it that one runs into in many spiritual circles these days, it represents the consequential future. It's the so-called "Law of Balance," the idea that as a person sows, so he will reap, and that one must exchange an eye for an eye or a tooth for a tooth. If I wrong you in some life, then I am tied to you (and you to me, for it's always reciprocal) energetically until I correct that wrong by doing something good for you in another life (or conversely, I suffer the same wrong that I did to you). Karma is the principle of consequence.

But one of the key teachings in Christianity is the power of grace and forgiveness. Grace and forgiveness can set us free of karma. If you wrong me and I forgive you, then you and I are free. You do not have to "pay me back" in some manner. Of course, you may have lessons to learn about wronging people, which is another matter—you can learn those lessons in any number of ways, and my act of forgiveness might be sufficient to enable you to do so. But as far as a consequential future goes, forgiveness is one of those creative acts, emerging from love, that can alter the course of events and bring something unexpected into being.

When I was a child, I used to love playing with a tether ball we had hanging from a pole in the playground of a park near where I lived. I would hit the ball and it would swing around and come back to me. This is a very simple system, and the action of the ball fully exemplified a consequential future. I knew that because of the tether, if I hit the ball, it would not fly off across the playground but it would come back. It was a very simple system.

A thermostat is a simple system. When I get up in the morning and turn on the heat, I know that barring some malfunction with the furnace or a loss of electricity, the heat will come on. And I know that the thermostat will keep the temperature regulated in the house according to simple principles of thermodynamics and homeostasis. There is a very clear line between cause and effect, action and consequence.

But the more complex the system becomes, the harder it can be to predict just what consequences will emerge from a particular action or input. More variables come into play. A human being is just such a complex system. If you hit me, I might behave like the tether ball and hit you back; but I might surprise you. I might turn the other cheek. I might bless and forgive you instead. You may think I'll behave in one way, but being a complex system, I may act differently from what you expect.

In many ways, the world is an even more complex system. We still don't fully understand it, any more than we fully understand ourselves. This is one reason the global warming debate has been so contentious. If the world acted like a tether ball, we could see clearly that if we hit the ball, the world's temperature will go up. But the world is more complex than a tether ball. Sometimes we do something, and the temperature does go up; sometimes we do something, and the temperature may go down. We may predict one thing, and something else occurs. Those who believe that global warming is occurring (and most scientists do because the bulk of the evidence, even allowing for anomalies tells us that it is) can find lots of consequences that point to a particular future. But there are those anomalies. The system doesn't always act as we think it should or would according to the models we've created to describe planetary behavior. When this happens, those who deny that global warming is happening have evidence to support their view of things.

The more complex the system—the less and less it's like a tether ball—the more we live with paradox and hypothesis. There are things we don't know, things we can't predict, and those things could make a difference we don't yet understand or perceive. This is no reason to deny what is happening, or what we think is happening. But it is a reason to be open to multiple possibilities.

Even more it's a reason not to limit our view of the future only to consequences and effects, however scary or powerful they may be. We want to be aware of them obviously and deal with them skillfully and as mindfully as we can, but we also want to be aware of the imaginal and creative futures as well. For there is where our power to change lies, and that is where hope lies as well.

Chapter Six
Miracles

I had been at the Findhorn Foundation community for four days when Peter Caddy, one of the three founders of the place, came up and asked if I'd like to go with him as he took an Anglican minister and his wife on a tour of the gardens.

Findhorn was famous for its miraculous garden. The community was situated on a beach and was often buffeted by cold, salty winds off the North Sea. It was not a hospitable site for growing a lush flower and vegetable garden, but nevertheless plants of all kinds grew there quite happily. Soil experts from a nearby university had come to investigate and had gone away puzzled. Their report said that soil conditions were such that none of the plants growing in the community should be doing so, yet there they were. And they weren't just surviving. They were vibrant with life and health, and a number of the vegetables were larger than even the local farmers could produce. The experts declared that there was some "Factor X" at work.

In time Peter and his two co-founders, his wife Eileen and their friend Dorothy Maclean revealed that the Factor X was their contact and cooperation with invisible beings and forces making up what Dorothy called "the Intelligence behind all of Nature." In effect, they were working with nature spirits and angel-like spiritual intelligences that Dorothy called Devas, a Sanskrit word meaning simply "Shining Ones."

When word of this got out, many people made the pilgrimage north to the Findhorn peninsula far in the north of Scotland about twenty-five miles east of Inverness to see this phenomenon. Some of them stayed, and in this way, the community began to expand. When I arrived in the summer of 1970, there were about nineteen permanent residents and about twice that number of guests and visitors. A year and a half later, there were a hundred and fifty residents, so quickly did the community grow.

Among the visitors who came each year were this Anglican minister and his wife. He cultivated roses as a hobby and was an expert in a wide variety of rose species. The previous year, in 1969, he had generously offered to use his knowledge and skill to landscape the community in roses. Now he had come back, and Peter wanted to show him how his flowers were doing.

The four of us set off on our tour. It did not take long as in those days the community was not very large, but as the tour progressed, I noticed the minister becoming more and more agitated. I couldn't understand why because the roses were magnificent. I'm not much of a botanist or a gardener—cell biology was my area of interest when I was in college—but even I could tell that these were very happy flowers, vibrant with color and energy. But the minister seemed unaccountably distressed.

When the tour was complete, we went back to Peter's bungalow for a cup of tea (this was Britain, after all) and a chat. That was when the minister confessed. It seemed that he felt the community's story of working with nature spirits and Devas was "pure poppycock," but his wife believed and dragged him north to Scotland every summer to spend their holiday at Findhorn. He hated it, but he couldn't convince his wife not to come. So the previous year he had decided to play a trick on Peter and the community. He had made his offer to plant roses and then selected types of roses he knew could not survive in the sandy, rocky soil of Findhorn or in the cold and windy weather of northern Scotland. He even selected some roses that only grew indoors in hothouses. Then he waited for this year's trip when he could show his wife all the dead roses, allowing him to convince her Findhorn's claims were all fantasy so they would stop coming to the community.

Instead he found his roses thriving, some of them even more so than in his own garden! It was, he said, a miracle, pure and simple.

Of course, no one in the community knew of the minister's scheme and dealt in good faith with the roses as they dealt with all the plants, with love and with communion and cooperation with the spirits of Nature. The results had been plain to see, and seeing them, the minister became an enthusiastic supporter of Findhorn and its work.

The Findhorn Foundation community had its beginnings in a trailer park, named the Findhorn Bay Caravan Site (*caravan* being what the British call a trailer). Located on a strip of land between Findhorn Bay and the Moray Firth, a large body of water opening into the North Sea, this trailer park mainly served holiday vacationers from Glasgow who would come up in the summer months to play on the beach. In the winter, many of the trailers were used by local servicemen stationed at the adjoining Royal Air Force base of Kinloss. I've seen pictures of this trailer park and the land it was on Peter Caddy and his family moved there in 1962 with their trailer. It is mostly gorse and broom, two hardy Scottish plants, and a kind of scrub grass—and sand. Looking at it, one might have imagined many things for its future but a lush, abundant almost Edenic garden of flowers, vegetables and trees, including some species that are normally found much further south in warmer, even tropical conditions, would not be one of them.

At the time Peter and his family and their friend and co-worker Dorothy moved there, they had just fallen off their own personal trampolines. Peter had managed a large, local hotel and Dorothy had been his secretary. Although in the years that he was manager, Peter had transformed this hotel from a two-star to a four-star rating, ongoing conflicts with management had led to his being fired. With no place to go and on welfare, the only place they had to live was a small trailer they owned, which they moved onto the Findhorn Bay Caravan Site. They imagined they would only be there a short time before Peter got a new job. But economic conditions were hard, and there were no jobs forthcoming. Days became weeks, weeks became months, and to supplement their diet, they started a garden on a patch of ground that was the garbage dump for the trailer park.

They were not very hopeful of the results, for none of them had any experience in gardening, particularly in the harsh conditions of a beach in northern Scotland. But they had another resource. Dorothy, Eileen and Peter had years of experience in meditation and tuning in to a spiritual source they called the "God Within." From this source, Dorothy was told there were spiritual intelligences within nature and that she should call upon them for help in growing the garden. She did, and the rest, as they say, is history.

Metaphorically, instead of collapsing when they fell off their personal trampolines, they soared. They discovered they had wings. They discovered they could participate in a miracle. They turned what could have been a disaster, being unemployed and homeless, into a new and unexpected future on a very unexpected place, and in the process they created a spiritual center that has been an inspiration throughout the world for nearly sixty years.

A friend of mine many years ago felt as if he had fallen off his own life's trampoline when he was diagnosed one day with a particular aggressive form of cancer. He underwent a variety of treatments but to no avail as the cancer spread throughout his body. Eventually, he was sent home to die. In this case, though, his home was in another country, so mutual friends of his and mine took him into their house where he could die in peace and comfort and surrounded with a loving atmosphere. He was only expected to live two or three days.

One evening, he lay on his bed drifting in and out of consciousness. His host and hostess had gone out briefly, so he was temporarily alone in the house. As he lay there, he was startled to see a figure, radiant with Light, walk through the door of his bedroom and stand beside his bed. He told me later he thought this was an angel come to take him across the threshold to the Post-Mortem Realms. But as I remember his story, this being came forward and entered his body, dissolving into him, and he felt his body turn into Light. He wasn't sure whether he was dreaming or awake, but he felt a new vitality in his body.

When his host and hostess returned, they found him up and about and bubbling with joy. He told them what had happened. As far as he could tell, he had been healed. Subsequent examinations in the hospital showed that indeed he was now cancer-free, having experienced what his doctors called a "spontaneous miraculous remission."

And here's another, similar story. A friend of mine, Dr. Lee Irwin, is a professor of religious studies at the College of Charleston in South Carolina and an acknowledged expert in both Native American spirituality and traditions and in the Western Esoteric traditions. He is well-versed in shamanic and mystical lore and in skills pertaining to each.

Lee was giving the final exam in one of his classes and noted that a young woman who had been one of his best students was unaccountably missing from the class. Then about halfway through the period, she showed up at the door and asked to speak to him privately. He met her out in the hallway, and he could see that she was distraught. She told him she had just come from a doctor's office where she had been told she had an inoperable and inevitably terminal form of cancer. The doctor had given her only a few months to live.

Without thinking, he spontaneously reached out and hugged her, something he normally would never do with a student, particularly a female one. He told me later she was stiff at first and then relaxed into his arms and just melted. As she did so, he said he felt a subtle energy pass between them. Then he released her and told her to go home and rest and not worry about the exam.

Later that evening when he was home, Lee began to feel sick himself. He didn't associate this with his student at first, but being knowledgeable about subtle energy process and the way in which a person with shamanic sensitivities can take on the illness of another, he went through a process of clearing and cleansing his own energy field until he felt better.

The following Monday, his class met for a final time to receive the results of their exams. To his surprise, the young woman showed up, smiling and joyous. When he asked her how she was, she said she'd just been to the doctor's office again, and new tests had shown she was entirely cancer free. "Somehow," she said, "the tumor disappeared over the weekend. The doctor says it's a miracle!"

Remembering the sickness he had felt the previous Friday evening, Lee realized that in true shamanic fashion, he had indeed taken her illness into himself and transmuted it, healing her in the process. "I'm sure," he told me later, "that if I hadn't taken action to clear and cleanse my own energy field, I might now be dealing with that cancer myself."

In all three of these stories, an expected future, a future that experts said was inevitable, didn't happen. Instead, a miracle happened. Something out of the ordinary and unpredicted happened. And when it did, everything changed. Flowers that were supposed to have died, lived. Two people who were terminally ill were cured and lived.

A consequential future was altered by something emerging from the creative future.

Take a moment just to appreciate this fact. For most of us, miracles are just fantasies or supernatural events that happened a long time ago and were recorded in sacred texts like the Bible. They have little place in the hard, cold reality of everyday life. And yet as a spiritual teacher, I see miracles happening in peoples' lives all the time. They may not be as dramatic as the three I described, though some are even more so, but in every case, a future was changed in unexpected ways.

The ability to create miracles lies in that place in us from which the creative future emerges. From my point of view, an important step in learning how to shape our future and meet the challenges before us is to open ourselves to this innate capacity to create, invoke or participate in miracles.

For many people this is an unfamiliar idea, even a nonsensical one. If they accept miracles at all, it's within a religious context in which they are supernatural events brought about by an intervention by God that suspends the natural order of things. Miracles are not events that we can create or whistle up to order.

I have no problem accepting the possibility of divine intervention or the actions of Intelligences and Presences from higher spiritual worlds whose impact in our world can seem mysterious but undeniable in its effects. I believe that some miracles do fall into this category and are the expression of consciousnesses acting for reasons far beyond human comprehension and in ways that transcend human capabilities.

But I do reject that such actions are "supernatural." Rather I see them as manifestations of principles of nature that we do not yet understand. There are many things that we take for granted in our world that would have seemed miraculous to our ancestors because they would not have understood the principles behind their operation. If I took an IPod back in time and played music or a movie on it for Julius Caesar, he would undoubtedly believe it a manifestation of magic and miracles. If I showed it to Benjamin Franklin, he might come closer to appreciating it as a technological artifact, but it would still seem miraculous. And yet I know that there is nothing magical or miraculous about it. The IPod most certainly is not a religious or spiritual manifestation (however highly Apple may think of it).

In a similar manner, miracles seem, well, miraculous to us because we don't understand the principles involved. But this doesn't mean we couldn't understand them. I believe that to do so, we need to approach them not as religious manifestations but as indicators of processes at work that are as natural in their sphere of operation as electromagnetism is in its. Such an exploration is beyond the scope of this little book. But in the three stories I told there is a clue that can start us down a path of understanding and which I believe is germane to the power to face and shape the future. In all three cases, a relationship was involved, one that held and allowed for the exchange of living energies. In all three cases, as well, love was present in one form or another.

In the case of Findhorn, plants didn't just automatically grow in the sandy soil of the beach. There was deliberate work and loving care put into the garden. But there was also an equally deliberate and conscious cultivation of a collaborative and loving relationship between the human gardeners and the nature spirits and Devas. A partnership was created, and that partnership generated a field of subtle energy that intensified the life force in and around the soil and the plants. It was this partnership that manifested the "Factor X" the soil experts could not explain.

In the case of Lee Irwin, he did not heal his student through a spontaneous act of giving her a sympathetic hug. For many years, he has trained himself in holding and working with subtle energies within and around his body through Tai Chi, Qi Gong, and other techniques, including meditation and mystical contemplation, as well as being versed in shamanic practices. While he doesn't present himself as a healer, he certainly carries vital subtle energies around him. Because of the spontaneous empathy and compassion he felt for his student when she revealed her devastating news, these subtle energies responded in a recognizably shamanic manner, healing the young woman by drawing the illness into himself and transmuting it. I know of shamanic practitioners who do this deliberately as healers; the only difference is that it happened to Lee spontaneously and without his conscious intent. But in that moment, he possessed the energy that could heal and through the compassionate feeling that linked him empathetically to his student, that energy *did* heal, allowing the "miracle" to take place.

And what about my other friend? I don't know all the details of his circumstances well enough to analyze it in this way. I know only what he and the other friends with whom he stayed—one of whom was a medical doctor—and in whose house this event took place, have told me. But I know the doctor and his wife as very loving and compassionate people. I have no doubt at all that in taking in our mutual friend for what they all believed were his last two or three days on earth, they did so with a great deal of love and created as supportive an environment for him as they could. Again, I don't know all the details, but knowing all involved, I am confident that their efforts generated a loving field of subtle energy that certainly contributed to the healing that took place. It fits patterns I have seen elsewhere and at other times, as well as information I have been given from colleagues in the subtle worlds about how these things can occur.

Of course, loving relationships and energetic partnerships are not the whole answer. By themselves they are not the Factor X for miracles, for there are many examples of loving relationships that while undoubtedly comforting and supportive for those involved still do not result in healings.

But as I said, it is a clue. Whatever happens or doesn't happen at other times and in other places and conditions, in these three examples a key element was a loving relationship and the creation of an energetic field and partnership, however briefly it might have existed. This field in turn had the capacity to receive and hold subtle energies in a manner sufficient for something extraordinary to take place. Because of that field and the energies that flowed into and through it, futures were changed.

And there's another clue. In these stories, no one was trying to make a miracle happen, not even at Findhorn. No one had any intentions or expectations. Lee wasn't trying to heal his student; he was as surprised as anyone when it occurred. My doctor friend and his wife weren't trying to heal our mutual friend of his cancer, either. They were thinking simply of creating a space in which he could have a good death.

And as for Findhorn, working with the nature spirits was part of the experiment of the place. It was one of the overall missions of the community, to demonstrate what could happen—what was possible—when human beings worked in cooperation with non-physical beings, particularly those related to the health and wellbeing of the natural environment. In the case of the roses, no one knew that none of these plants were supposed to live. They didn't know that the Anglican minister had deliberately sabotaged his gift to prove Findhorn's assertions incorrect. So no one was trying to "heal" the roses or keep them alive or overcome the minister's duplicity. The roses were simply part of the garden, and the garden as a whole was being held and tended in a loving energetic field of cooperation and attunement.

Thus no one was trying to produce a specific consequence. No one was envisioning a future in which people and roses were healed. Not that they couldn't have done so, and perhaps such intent would have worked as well. But in these three cases, whatever the "Factor X" was that was at work, it did not come from an effort to change a consequential future. But these miracles do manifest the power of the creative future, the place from which unexpected possibilities emerge, often triggered by love and compassion or, in Findhorn's case, by an imagination of possibility and openness to a larger, more holistic conception of reality.

This is an important clue. It tells us that the future arises not just from causes in the past acting in a linear way to produce effects; it arises not just as a predictable expression of consequences, but as part of a deeper, more comprehensive ecology of time, one that includes the power of consciousness with its ability to create surprises.

Facing the Future

Chapter Seven
An Ecology of Time

When we read about the implications of peak oil or of climate change, when we see the inability of leaders to wisely lead due to political gridlock and irrational partisanship, when we view the destruction in lives caused by terrorism and cultural intolerance, or feel the effects upon the wellbeing of our towns and neighborhoods, our businesses and our jobs from malfeasance and greed on the part of large corporations and financial institutions, we might be forgiven for thinking, "Only a miracle can save us!"

From one perspective, such a statement might be taken as a sign of despair and of giving up in hopelessness. It can be seen as an admission of powerlessness before an onrushing future of one disaster after another. But from another perspective, this is a powerful and creative insight. To craft a positive future, something is needed that goes beyond the normal way of viewing reality, and in particular beyond our usual conception of time and the consequential future. We need a new way of seeing and thinking.

Again I come back to the question I asked in an earlier chapter, "What is time? What is the future?" At the moment, one understanding of time and of the future burdens and frightens us with images of inevitable catastrophes and loss while another constrains our ability to adapt to changing conditions by blinkering us with images of inevitable progress. In both cases it is the notion of inevitability, of time moving in a straight and unyielding line, that limits us. We think of time as a road or as a river. We need instead to think of it as an ecology.

For many years I was in communication and partnership with a non-physical being whom I called "John." He was a mentor, a friend, and a colleague engaged in a collaborative enterprise that I shall describe in the next chapter. In our work together, the subject of prophecy occasionally came up, in particular because for the most part John refused to engage in it. This was not because he was unable to do so. There were times when he felt it important to say something about future events he could see unfolding, and he was amazingly accurate. He predicted the arising of Jihadist terrorism in the Islamic world some ten years before Al Qaeda appeared on the scene and said it would become a major threat to the world if steps were not taken to ameliorate or solve the Israeli-Palestinian conflict. Likewise, John predicted the collapse and disappearance of the Soviet Union six years before it took place and described exactly how it would come about.

But such predictions were rare. When I asked him why, he said, "If I tell you what the future holds, you see it as an event, and you look only in its direction. But the future is unfolding all around you; it comes from all directions. It's far better to be mindful and alert to the present that surrounds you, otherwise you may be blindsided by events that you were not expecting simply because you became fixated upon a particular prophecy." Later he said, "Time is not what you think it is. It is not a road running through a landscape; it is the landscape itself. Your presence in that landscape is like a seed from which the future grows. Time holds and nurtures the seeds of possibility in you and in all living beings and in consciousness itself, and from these seeds come the future you experience. To know the future, you must know yourselves. In many ways, your consciousness *is* your future. This is true for you as a person and it is true collectively for humanity as a whole."

John was a being who saw everything in terms of wholes and wholeness. He had a holistic consciousness, one very aware of patterns, relationships, and interconnections. For him time was not one thing but many things all acting together, all in relationship. The future was not something that didn't exist yet but an element within the "landscape of time" or what I've come to think of as the "ecology of time." For John, it was not so much that everything was happening simultaneously or that there was no time; he felt that the idea of an "eternal Now" in which there was no past or future but only the present was simplistic and a product of human thought not fully grasping the nature of a holistic, multidimensional reality. Instead, time was a complex topology in which past, present, and future were not in a linear relationship but in a collaborative and mutually interactive one.

This is not how we popularly think of time or of the future. In my own work and through my interaction and collaboration with beings like John, I have learned to experience time somewhat as they do, or at least to understand their point of view. (I say "somewhat" because I think I would need to be a non-physical, "hyperdimensional" being like they are in order to fully or truly experience time as they do; as a physical person, I am still constrained by the way my brain and earthly consciousness processes time.) It is definitely not the same as "timelessness" or the timeless state that mystics often experience and describe. I have experienced that as well and know the difference. There is no loss of past or future; they are not subsumed into an eternal Present. Rather they are presences that manifest energy. Both are fluid and malleable and represent various states of probability pushing to manifest. In a sense, there are many futures, each an "energy presence" or "energy complex" reaching back "through time" if I think of time as a linear road, or acting as part of the landscape of time if I think of it that way, to influence what actually happens. We get a glimmer of this in the idea of "self-fulfilling prophecies," but that idea usually represents a psychological phenomenon more than an energetic one.

However, psychology and more recently neurobiology offers a complementary insight into the malleability of time. We think of memory as the storing of data in the mind and the brain. This data tells us what happened in the past, and when we have a linear view of time, this past is over and done with; it cannot be altered. Omar Khayyam, the Eleventh Century Persian mathematician, astronomer and poet wrote:

An Ecology of Time

The Moving Finger writes; and, having writ,
Moves on: nor all thy Piety nor Wit
Shall lure it back to cancel half a Line,
Nor all thy Tears wash out a Word of it.

But modern brain research suggests this is not entirely true. I'm not speaking here of losing one's memory or forgetting. Rather, each time we remember it's as if the brain is forming the appropriate synapses for the first time; it's as if we are experiencing the event for the first time. We aren't "remembering" so much as we are "reconstructing." The brain, as I understand it from a friend who is a neuroscientist studying these things, constantly reforms memory: the "Moving Finger" writes and then writes it all again, and sometimes it doesn't rewrite it exactly as it was written before.

We are all too familiar with how memory can play us false. We think we remember an event and then discover that what we remember isn't precisely what happened. This is not simply due to faulty memory; it's due to the fact that we remember through our emotions and thoughts. And a memory is more than just data stored about the past; it's not like information I have on my hard drive in my computer which will be the same whenever I retrieve it. Memory is also a presence of energy that affects and shapes us in the moment

Many therapeutic approaches are based on this fact. We don't erase the actual event. If I was beaten by my father, then I was beaten by my father (I wasn't, by the way). But the memory of those beatings as an effect in my life, as a force of living energy within me, can be changed, even erased. The past as part of my internal landscape of consciousness alters. What was once a mountain now becomes a level plain, losing its power to challenge and torment me. The substance of the land—the action of the beatings—is still there, but it has been reconfigured in a way that changes the topology of time within me. The "Moving Finger" may have moved on, but the writing it left behind is now in a different font, one that doesn't affect me in the same way.

This example doesn't "prove" the perspective John had about time as a landscape or as an ecology. I use it mainly as a metaphor or as a beginning step into the experience of reality that John had. For him, the past and future both existed as probabilities, not as certainties. A past event for John had a very high probability of existence, but difficult as it may be for us to grasp from our perspective, it was not one hundred percent. And by probability, John meant a measure of the power that an event (which he saw as a configuration of energy) had to manifest itself.

At 4:00 am on March 28, 1979, the partial core meltdown in the nuclear reactor at Three Mile Island in Pennsylvania began. The accident was contained and the process halted before a full meltdown and nuclear catastrophe occurred. Some years earlier in the late Sixties, I had had an experience of seeing through my subtle awareness an image of such an accident in an American nuclear reactor. In addition to the image itself, I felt this event as a particular configuration of energy—that is to say, it had an certain "flavor" about it, a certain vibration of subtle energies that was recognizable. When I asked John about it, he said that it was a probability that was working its way down towards manifestation in the physical plane. If nothing happened to divert or diffuse it, he said, there probably would be such a nuclear accident in the United States. In those days, I did not have much understanding of what I now call subtle activism, so I didn't know just what to do about this other than to ask for whatever spiritual help was available to mitigate or prevent this accident.

The years passed and nothing happened, so I forgot about it. Then in early March of 1979, the movie *The China Syndrome* with Jack Lemmon was released, and I went to see it. The movie was about an accident that causes a core meltdown in an American nuclear reactor and the catastrophe that follows. Seeing the movie, I remembered my vision of some years earlier, but I thought no more about it than that.

Then twelve days later, the accident at Three Mile Island took place. Watching the news reports, I was struck by an inner perception that the subtle energies surrounding this event were identical to the ones I had seen years before in my vision. Three Mile Island was the probabilistic event I had seen moving towards manifestation in the physical world. But it was nowhere near as devastating as what I had seen in the vision. I asked John, and he said, "The energy surrounding this event found release and expression through human consciousness as a result of the movie that you saw. It did not need to take full physical manifestation in order to raise awareness of the dangers and risks in the way you are handling nuclear power. In effect, the movie and the accident were part of the same manifestation, the one mitigating and lessening the other."

In other words, the event I saw years earlier was not simply a physical event destined to happen in the consequential future. It was an event in the *landscape of time*, of which human consciousness is a part, and not just on some linear road of time.

I don't wish to enter into a metaphysical discourse on the cosmology and nature of time here; that requires a different kind of book than this one. But it is important that we have a sense of time as an ecology of contributing and interactive forces if we are to understand how we might face the future with grace and creative power. If I think of the future as a road and large, destructive events are rolling down this road towards me, I can become despairing and fearful for I know of no other place to be but on the road, waiting to be crushed into the pavement. But if I see time as an ecology, unfolding as an interaction between various elements, then I can realize that I am one of the contributing elements. I'm not all powerful, but I'm not a helpless victim either. I can participate, and perhaps my participation will be part of the Factor X that brings a miracle into being—and a miracle may simply be our term for when we experience the holistic landscape of time and not just the linear road of time.

The ecology of time includes at least the following elements: what we call the past, present, and future as probabilistic energy fields, our personal and collective consciousnesses, the consciousness of the world and of nature, the participation of the subtle worlds (which I'll discuss in the next chapter), and the energy released by our actions. It is in the space created by the interaction of all of these that miracles can arise; it is certainly in this space that the future unfolds and manifests as an expression of this ecology.

Thinking of time in this way is certainly unusual. It can also be challenging, for we are not accustomed in our culture to thinking in holistic ways. We are straight-line people, thinking in linear terms of cause and effect. And as I said in a previous chapter, where simple systems are involved, like tether balls, such thinking is very effective. But life, the planet, our selves, and time are not simple systems. They are complex, highly interactive and holistic. We intuitively know this is so, but we still try to reduce them down to the tether ball level of interaction.

One place where this happens is with the art of manifestation. Manifestation is the study of techniques that use states and processes of consciousness to influence and shape physical events in seemingly miraculous ways. It is precisely a way of trying to shape the future using "inner" or non-physical means, a topic very germane to this book. In one way or another, through our thoughts and actions, we are always trying to manifest individually and collectively a future that we deem will be positive and happy.

Manifestation—or as I prefer to call it, "life-shaping"—is a complex interaction between consciousness, time, and the world around us. Popular books like *The Secret* present it as a form of positive thinking and affirmation, using the "law of attraction" to bring to you what you want. Think positively, and you will get positive things; think negatively, and you will get negative events in your life. What could be simpler to understand and use?

But this is the tether-ball level of description, turning a complex set of relationships within an ecology of mind and being into a simplistic linear process. It's like using the rules for tether ball in all circumstances. If I'm on a tether ball court, this will work, but if I'm on a basketball court, it won't, and life is a lot more like basketball than tether ball. Manifestation is more accurately seen as a process of incarnation—of being and becoming and of how we express ourselves in the wholeness of our lives on earth—than as one of attraction.

There is a principle of attraction that works in life, but it's hardly a "law" like the law of gravity or the laws of thermodynamics. My father believed in manifestation. In fact, he and my mother were married by Dr. Norman Vincent Peale, the minister of the Marble Collegiate Church in New York City and the prophet of positive thinking. But Dad was what's known as a "worry-wart." If something bad could happen in the future, Dad worried about it. He often said he provided a pessimistic "balance" to Mom's bright optimism. If there really was a "law of attraction," Dad should have been visited by one disaster after another; he certainly imagined them. He should have been the poster child of how not to manifest.

But in fact, none of Dad's worries ever came to pass, and in fact, he was a very good manifestor, with many good things happening to him throughout his long life. The reason was simple. He could indulge in so-called negative and fearful thinking and imagining, but in all his relationships with people, he was loving, compassionate, giving, outgoing, and positive. He traveled widely, spoke five or six languages fluently and could get by in several others, and was always seeking out people of different cultures and backgrounds to learn from. He genuinely loved and respected people, and feeling that, they loved him back. Good things flowed to him not because he was a positive thinker; Dr. Peale, who wrote *The Power of Positive Thinking*, would have been disappointed in him on that score. They flowed to him because he was a positive being, a person of love and goodwill who was always concerned for the wellbeing and welfare of those around him.

Positive thinking is often suggested as an antidote to negative images of the future. If you suggest that the future may be less than rosy and may in fact contain some real challenges and difficulties, you can be accused to "thinking negatively." Be positive, you're told, and all will turn out well.

Positive thinking would be a wonderful thing if in fact there were any actual thinking involved with it. But all too often, the "thinking" part boils down to simply—and obsessively—holding positive, bright, happy images in one's mind. There's no real critical or creative thinking going on at all. It would be more accurate to call this technique "positive unconsciousness."

We get nowhere by denying problems. If a woodcarver discovers that there's an imperfection in the piece of wood he's using, by acknowledging and studying it, he may find a way of incorporating it into the carving itself. Something emerges that is whole and beautiful, whereas if he'd ignored the imperfection or pretended it wasn't there, the wood might have split and become useless. We do neither reality nor the future any favors by pretending negative consequences to past actions are not possible; all we do is diminish our mindfulness, our awareness, and our capacity to shape the future in more holistic ways. We dumb down and narrow our consciousness in the process of denial so that we become less effective.

But there is an even more important reason why denial or rejection of unpleasant images may hinder us, assuming we do not become pathologically fearful and obsessed with them.

I was once talking with a non-physical being, not John but another of the colleagues I work with in the subtle worlds. I asked him about powers, such as the power to heal or the power to manifest. As a teacher, I wanted more insights and information on how one might develop such things and how I might teach them. His response was unexpected. "There are no "powers," he said. "There are only relationships."

For me, this was an immensely helpful perspective. We are always forming relationships with each other, with events, with places and situations. Rather than thinking, "How can I bring a healing power into this situation," I would instead ask, "How might I form a healing relationship with this situation?" This is a profound difference, for the implication of power is that it is something we have that we use to do something in the world, to affect another, to make something happen, and so forth. We are the agency acting upon the circumstances and people around us. But a relationship is something we form together. It is co-creative. It is a partnership.

Actually, this perspective shouldn't have surprised me, as my inner colleagues are always stressing the importance of partnership and the need for a "partnership cosmology" or a "partnership ecology."

But it fits with the miracles I described in the last chapter. Findhorn formed a three-way relationship between the human beings, the subtle worlds, and the plants in the garden, and miracles happened. Lee formed a relationship of empathy and compassion with his student, and healing took place. The doctor and his wife formed a relationship of love and support with my friend, and he was healed. In all cases, relationships were formed rather than powers being exerted; through those relationships an energetic and loving field came into being, even if only for an instant, and change took place.

If I view time as an ecology, as a set of relationships, then I don't want to deny or turn away from relationships I may form with the present or the past or future just because I don't like the images they're presenting. The "power" to transform the past, the present, or the future lies in my capacity to form a transformative relationship with them. It's by accepting what's there that I gain the means to engage with it and perhaps change it.

In this process, I want to understand that the images of the future that I hold or that others present to me are only part of the interrelationships from which the actual, experienced future will emerge. I can imagine what tomorrow may be like, but I haven't experienced it yet. And the experience may turn out to be different than what I'm expecting.

This is the point of seeing it as an ecology, and the reason John refused to make prophecies. The "revealed" or experienced future is the product of a number of factors all interacting with each other: the past, the present, the images of the future, the inertia or momentum of events leading to certain consequences, our consciousness, the quality of our beingness, our actions, our relationships, the fields of subtle energy we create, and so on. Simply sharing an image of the future in the form of a prophecy doesn't begin to cover the complexity of this ecology of interrelationships and variables.

Furthermore, in this ecology, I am an actor. I can contribute, for I am part of the consciousness and subtle energy of the world and of humanity. I may be a small part, but I'm a part nonetheless.

In a simple tether-ball, linear system, energy input equals energy output; action equals consequence. If I hit the ball hard, it will spin around and come back at me hard. If I hit the ball softly, it will move only a small amount and may not spin around and come back to me at all.

But in a complex system, we are dealing with non-linear

dynamics in which the relationship between input and output can be counterintuitive. A small input may have a huge effect; this is the idea behind the notion that the fluttering of a butterfly's wings in China can cause a hurricane in the Atlantic. Conversely, a large impact may disperse quickly through the system and have little effect at all.

The ecology of time—indeed, the ecology of life, being, and consciousness itself here on earth—is a non-linear dynamical system. This is why each person is important, because any of us at any time through our actions or our thoughts might just be the butterfly whose wings change the world.

This is what happened to the poet Gary Snyder. In the summer of 1971, he was backpacking in the mountains of California. One night he was sitting alone by his campfire when a stranger showed up, another hiker. He invited him to join them, and the two of them spent several hours talking over the crucial issues of the day, the Vietnam War, peace, activism, and the responsibility that citizens owe the nation. Finally, they went to sleep. When Snyder awoke the next morning, he found the man was gone, but he had left a note. It thanked Gary for helping him come to a decision and to keep an eye on the newspapers as he would be seeing the result of their talk soon. A few days later the New York Times released the first of the secret documents that became known as the Pentagon Papers, given to the newspaper by Daniel Ellsberg. These papers created a furor, led to Congressional investigations into the war, to street protests, and eventually to ending the war. This was a huge wave of change, and it was set into motion that night around the campfire, for the stranger who sat and talked with Snyder was Daniel Ellsberg struggling with the decision of whether or not to release the documents he had to the newspapers.

This was a physical meeting between two strangers, but from my perspective there can be meetings of energy and consciousness as well, invisible to the eye but no less potent. Somewhere in the world a man or woman or a team of people may be on the brink of making a discovery that will revolutionize physics or chemistry and totally transform our energy situation for the better. All they need is a little push of energy to make the necessary conceptual breakthrough, and that push might come from you, from your positive beingness, from your consciousness interacting creatively with the ecology of time and spreading throughout the subtle fields of the planet as a force of inspiration.

The ecology of time says change is possible in ways we may not imagine, that miracles can happen, and that we can be their source.

Chapter Eight
Invisible Friends

When I am asked if I have hope for humanity and for our future, I always say yes. The reason is because of humanity's invisible friends.

To understand this and why it gives me confidence, you need to accept as a working hypothesis that our world has another half, an invisible, non-physical half, that I call the subtle worlds (or sometimes, earth's "second ecology"). This is a challenging idea for many in our highly materialistic modern culture, but this other half of the world and the beings that inhabit it have been an experienced reality for most of humanity throughout all of our history. It is this other half of the world that the Findhorn Foundation community, for example, works with in producing the miracle of its garden, but they are hardly alone in recognizing the existence of the subtle dimensions. Millions of people have had, are having or will have experiences of non-physical beings and forces—after all, acknowledging and working with angels and other spiritual forces are a staple in most mystical, shamanic and religious beliefs and practices around the world. The fact that our physical science has yet to discover how to detect or measure these subtle realms doesn't mean they don't exist.

I have been aware of these subtle realms and of non-physical beings all my life. As I child, I thought everyone shared that awareness with me, and in fact, a great many children do. In our culture, though, this awareness doesn't often survive into adulthood. In my case, I was fortunate. The awareness itself was very strong, and I had support in exploring and developing it from my parents.

The subtle worlds are even more vast and diverse than the physical world. Describing them is far beyond the scope of this book, though if you are interested in pursuing the subject, you could start with my book *Subtle Worlds: An Explorer's Field Notes*. But they are vital contributors to the future of the planet; they are another element contributing to the outcomes unfolding within the ecology of time.

Not all non-physical beings are interested in humanity or our future; indeed, many subtle beings don't even know we exist or know very little about us. Whether we succeed as a species or end up destroying ourselves and becoming extinct makes little difference to them. But there are a great many other beings—including humans who are currently not in incarnation in the physical world—who are concerned, who do wish us to succeed, and who have only our highest good in their hearts and minds. They are truly our invisible friends, and they are engaged in a collective undertaking to ensure not just the survival but the evolutionary fulfillment of humanity—and indeed of all beings upon the earth.

Put simply, this undertaking is an effort to increase and enhance connections and relationships, both "horizontally" within the physical world and "vertically" between the physical and the subtle worlds. It is an expression of what I call *holopoiesis*, the impulse to create wholeness within a system. It does not matter whether the system is a single human being or the planet as a whole. A system that is integrated, coherent and whole is far more able to express its inherent potentials and capacities than one that is riven with internal divisions and incoherency and thus is unable to "get it together." For many subtle beings with whom I have worked, this is not a "spiritual" matter but one of energy efficiency. A system that is not whole in itself and connected harmoniously with its environment can be a source of blockage, obstruction, wasted energy, and the development of toxic situations. Again, this is true whether the system in question is a person, a town, a physical environment such as a pond or a forest, a corporation, a nation, or species, or a planet.

Without putting too fine a point on it, as individuals, in our relationships with each other, and in our relationships with the world, we are far from a state of wholeness. This is one reason we're facing such a set of scary images of the future. Both individually and collectively, we are often obstructions to the clean and life-affirming flow of energy in the world and all too often, because of that, we are sources of energetic and psychic pollution and toxicity as well as the physical variety.

This specifically is the problem the subtle worlds are seeking to solve.

But how does one become integrated and whole? It's not a mystical process. Wholeness is an emergent property, appearing as the elements of a system are able to connect, engage and work together in coherent and integrated ways. My wholeness emerges as my mind, body, emotions, and spirit are able to connect and enhance each other. There's wholeness in my marriage as my wife and I are able to connect, engage and enhance each other. There's wholeness in my neighborhood and town when different citizens and groups of citizens connect and work together in mutually supportive ways. Wholeness emerges from relationship, and a *holopoietic* strategy focuses on relationship.

It also focuses on intention, for while connections and relationships leading to wholeness can develop spontaneously, in many cases they need an energetic push. There often needs to be attention given to the possibilities and opportunities for such connections and an intention to make them happen, especially with complex systems like ourselves with strong boundaries and many differences between us. So holopoiesis is the intent to form wholeness-producing relationships and conditions.

In recent years as global travel and communications have increased, especially with the implementation of the Internet, much has been said about humanity becoming a "global brain" and a "nervous system" for Gaia, the spirit of the world as a living being in itself. Various writers have said that we are the means through which the world becomes "self-conscious" and "self-aware." This may make us feel good but from my experience with the subtle worlds, it's not true. Gaia doesn't need us to have a global brain or a nervous system nor to become self-aware. In its own way and using its own resources, it's quite aware and conscious, thank you very much. To imagine otherwise is a human conceit based on projecting our kind of consciousness as the standard by which all consciousness and awareness is measured.

On the other hand, the marvel of the Internet and the other technological developments that are increasingly wiring humanity into a humming, buzzing wholeness are very important for the enhancement of a *human* species global awareness and the development of our own planetary relationships, integration and wholeness. Gaia may not need it, but we surely do, and this level of technological achievement has a great deal of support from the non-physical worlds.

Humanity is not nearly as important to the world in the ways we like to think, based on our high estimations of our rational consciousness and intellectual prowess, but we are very important in ways that in our culture at least we haven't valued as highly. Essentially, our importance arises from our power to love and through that love to form relationships and connections that cross species boundaries. All beings are capable of love, but here in the physical world at least, we are capable of loving in a way that not only can create wholeness for ourselves but which can extend that to include others very different from who and what we are. We have the power of imaginative love, the capacity to enhance love through the power of imagination, understanding and empathy in a way that creates synthesis. It's not our minds that are important, at least not primarily; it's our hearts.

It comes back to the power of relationships and the way they create fields of energy that in turn can invoke and hold powerful subtle energies. Anyone can form surface relationships and connections; we do it all the time. But through our imaginations—through our power to step out of ourselves, to "shape-shift" into the form and life of another, to "walk a mile in another's shoes"—we can deepen those connections and relationships through understanding in ways that allow a mutually supportive and enhancing energy to flow between us. And when that happens, a mutual field comes into being—what I think of as a "partnership field"—that is stronger than what we could create or maintain on our own, one that can in turn receive and sustain more powerful subtle energies, which in turn further enhance the capacity for loving, for connecting, and for holopoiesis.

This is not an uncommon experience among individuals. It's less common between nations and groups, and it's even less common at the moment in our industrial civilization between humanity and the other non-human lives that share this world with us. Our partners and allies in the subtle worlds are focused on making this a more common experience for all across the board.

The wholeness that results when deeper relationships are formed is not simply a mystical phenomenon. The beings whom I know who are helping us are not particularly interested in mysticism or mystical experiences. They are more pragmatic. They see wholeness in terms of energy flow and efficiency, much like engineers evaluating an electrical system for how well it works.

Here's an example of what I mean. When I am writing, it's largely a solitary effort. Most of the time, the words flow comfortably well from mind to finger and into my computer. But there are times—more than I'd like—when the flow stops. I get stuck. At such times I can sit and mull over the problem, trying to think my way through it, but I know from experience that this will only be partially successful and more often than not simply leads to frustration and weariness

My other alternative is to find someone—usually my wife, Julia—and talk over the problem. After all, there's a reason people say that "two heads are better than one." And in our talking, I can feel energy start to flow again; I can feel ideas sparking in my mind. Inevitably, one of these sparks will ignite my creative engine and I'm up and moving again, the ideas and words flowing once more.

We've all had this experience. It's not at all uncommon; it's the principle behind brainstorming.

So, from the point of view of those in the subtle worlds who are seeking to help us (at least those with whom I'm in contact), wholeness is a way of increasing the generation and flow of creative energy. It makes for a richer, more durable and efficient energy system. Furthermore, it strengthens an energy system so that it can hold more than it might otherwise. I think of it this way: if a cup is cracked, it may shatter and fall apart when I pour hot coffee in it, but if it's whole and maintains its integrity (its state of molecular integration), it will receive that coffee and hold it without spilling.

The human species is cracked at the moment, and it is made up of cracked individuals. This is one of the problems the subtle worlds are addressing.

The physical world and its biosphere can be understood as a vast energy system that acts like a cup. Humanity is part of that cup. The subtle worlds are a different, more complex and intense energy system. They're like the hot coffee. The more the former can receive and hold the subtle energies of the latter without cracking and spilling, the more whole and integrated the earth can be. The subtle worlds wish to share their stimulating and life-giving energies; the physical world wishes to receive it and be enhanced by it, as well as giving those subtle energies expression they won't have otherwise. Both halves of the earth have a need for each other.

Think of the coffee and the cup. The hot coffee in the coffeepot is not doing anyone any good unless they can drink it, and for that, they need a cup. The cup by itself just sits on the desk and has nothing to offer except perhaps a space in which to put pencils and paper clips. But if you bring the coffee and the cup together, they complement each other. The cup lets the coffee be drunk and enjoyed, the coffee gives the cup a chance to express its nature and its usefulness as a container.

The relationship between the physical and subtle worlds is far more complex than that between coffee and a cup, but the principle is much the same. They are in a relationship which, as it deepens and expands, can benefit both sides and allow potentials to emerge that neither can express on its own. But the challenge is to deepen that relationship without cracking the cup or spilling the coffee. And for that to happen, humanity needs to find a greater degree of integration and wholeness. Individuals within humanity need to find a greater degree of integration and wholeness. And humanity needs to find a greater degree of integration and wholeness between itself and the rest of the world. We need to heal the cracks that we experience.

The key to this is love.

The subtle worlds in various ways have been trying to teach and inspire humanity, both individually and collectively, to understand and express love for millennia. This is a very ancient project! Are we any closer to success now?

Well, to watch the evening news one would be strongly tempted to say no. But my colleagues in the subtle worlds have a different view. They are very positive about where we are and where we're going.

To understand this, we need to see things from their point of view, part of which is influenced by the fact that they live in a very different time scale from us. What are a mere few decades of turmoil and difficulty if humanity comes out very much better at the other end in, say, a couple hundred years or so? If industrial civilization collapses due to overshooting our non-renewable resources and if we go through a small ice age or a rising of the sea levels due to climate changes, it's all grist for the mill if at the end of a thousand years we emerge wiser with a culture that is holistic, earth-attuned, and, to use John Michael Greer's phrase, "eco-technic." I have met beings in the subtle worlds who think exactly this way and can't quite understand what all the fuss is about when we get upset over the potential difficulties in the near future if the end result down the line will be a good one.

In effect, because of the ends they have in mind, they evaluate situations differently than I might. For example, there are subtle beings that have been fostering the development and growth of mutli-national corporations. I might see many of these corporations in their greed and their "translegality" (that is, their ability to act beyond the law of a particular nation because they exist within many nations with different legal systems and regulations) as a source of many of the problems we have in the world. But to my inner colleagues they are an important evolutionary driver for human consciousness, enabling connections between people across national and ethnic boundaries. As one of my contacts once said, "At one time it took war to enable peoples of different cultures and outlooks to discover each other and make connections, but now this can happen more peacefully within the operations of one of these corporations."

Thinking about this, I am reminded of our own history here in the United States. At the time of our Revolution, the original thirteen colonies were in effect thirteen different nations with different laws, different economies, different currencies, and different customs. At the time, the only national institution that allowed a person to experience being an "American" rather than a Pennsylvanian, a North Carolinian, or a New Yorker was the Continental Army. Men from all the Colonies served in this institution and got to know each other; connections and relationships were formed, and it was on the foundation of these relationships that the new nation developed.

Many of the efforts of the subtle worlds are focused on humanity developing a species-wide consciousness of connectedness and wholeness. It's about human wholeness, not just British or Chinese, South African or Algerian, Israeli or Iranian, American or Russian wholeness. The two world wars of the last century certainly brought people of different nationalities together, enabling people to travel, meet and work alongside people of other cultures; they formed connections, but at enormous cost in lives and destruction. Multinational corporations are doing much the same thing but without the bloodshed.

Even more important in this regard in fostering planetary connections and relationships is the effect of global travel and tourism and planetary communications through cell phones and the Internet. Industrial civilization and its modern electronic technological offshoot has been an important part of enabling a network of new global connections to develop. Even as I write this, amazing and unprecedented webs of relationships are being formed between people around the world who have never met each other physically but are nonetheless experiencing each other and collaborating as part of a global network of friendship, collegiality and consciousness. My own Internet classes are a modest example of this as students from different nations come together with me and with each other to explore new visions of spirituality.

For that matter, the emergence of cyberspace as a non-physical realm in which increasingly people are living their lives, doing business, forming friendships, finding entertainment, and learning new things has made my own work as a spiritual teacher so much easier. Computer-moderated virtual reality and cyberspace are not identical to the subtle worlds but there are significant parallels—such as their non-physicality and their comparative freedom from time and space—that I can use to illustrate some of the characteristics of "walking the worlds" between the different dimensions in the subtle worlds. I find that as people become increasingly accustomed to this invisible world of cyberspace growing alongside us, they gain the imaginative power to appreciate and feel into the unseen, non-physical world that has always been there as well. For people raised in a predominantly materialistic worldview, this can be immensely helpful.

The efforts of the subtle worlds of which I'm aware are focused on two objectives. One focuses on the empowerment of the capacity of the individual and the cultivation of individual freedom to use those capacities. In fact, this has largely been my own work, expressed through the development of what I call an "incarnational spirituality" that honors and finds spiritual resources within our individuality and personality. The second part deals with the intention and ability of individuals to connect and form the relationships that can lead to larger wholes being formed and a spirit of wholeness emerging.

I see both of these directions manifested in my kids and others of their generation. My kids, three of whom are in their twenties while one is a teenager, are increasingly part of a world of social networks in which the connections are largely electronic and mediated through their cell-phones, Ipods, and computers. For them, the relationships they are forming, and they can be with people anywhere in the world, are very real. Virtual communities are just as valuable and powerful for them as physical ones. They naturally think in connected and holistic ways that people of my generation have had to struggle to learn and appreciate. At the same time, because so much of this technology is interactive, they and many others of their generation are finding ways of being creative and of interacting with their world that is deeply empowering to their individuality. The tools they work with help them express their uniqueness in the midst of their connectedness.

I do not want to overromanticize this. All of these tools and technologies have their downsides. Industrial civilization and multi-national corporations, for instance, continue to impact the world in ways that are bringing us to the destructive, apocalyptic future that nobody in their right mind really wants. And in its allure, virtual technology can lead individuals away from expression of their unique personhood and into abstracted and disassociated states. A disdain can exist for the "meat world" of physical reality that works against incarnation and the blessing of the world.

This is the challenge faced by our friends and allies in the subtle worlds. Human beings in their "cracked" state can use any tool, any development, in a cracked way that ends up distorting its potential and creating further toxic conditions. It's enough to make a "subtle energy engineer" working with the evolution of human consciousness tear his or her hair out—if he or she had hair....

The beings of the subtle worlds can be powerful—after all, they include Archangels and Angels, Devas and other great planetary beings in their number—but they are neither omniscient nor omnipotent. They cannot wave a wand and have events and conditions manifest on earth just as they would want. They are not magical. They are lifeforms, consciousnesses and intelligences like you and me though existing in a very different mode of being; being non-physical really does make a significant difference, particularly in the experience of time. Because of these differences, they can make mistakes, and they do. They can suffer the effects of unintended consequences as well.

This is due in part to the necessity much of the time of working in tandem and partnership with a physical person or group in order to create a field of energy that can span both realms and bridge the differences. If the individual or individuals in question cannot handle the relationship or the energy involved, this can produce problems down the line. If I am "cracked" in my energy system, not as integrated and whole as I could be, then it's possible the more intense energy from a spiritual being can widen that crack, making me even less integrated and less whole. This is exactly like a cup shattering when hot coffee is poured into it. The results can range from simple personality difficulties for the individual involved (including ego inflation and a disconnection from others) to much wider consequences involving many people, perhaps even a whole nation, perhaps even the world. What may have started out as a viable, benign plan to give help to some part of humanity turns into something else, perhaps its opposite, becoming a force of destruction, much to the distress of the subtle beings involved.

There is a discipline to working with the subtle worlds, one that is grounded in love and its development and expression but also in honoring and strengthening one's individuality—making the cup stronger so it can hold the coffee. Part of the efforts of our invisible allies is to help modern humanity recognize and learn that discipline so that partnering with the subtle worlds can take place more safely and effectively.

I began this chapter saying that much of my hope for the future comes from my contact with the subtle worlds and from a recognition of the love and compassion they have for us, as well as a desire to see humanity succeed. I'm aware of the immense amount of blessing, healing, and inspiration coming from these non-physical dimensions to help humanity at this time. Not all of it is getting through, and some of it that does gets distorted, but still progress is being made. There are connections where there were none before, there are relationships where there were none before, there are new ideas, new visions, new insights that didn't exist before, and there's a growing awareness of the nature of the global problems that wasn't there before. For all their faults—and they are many—industrial civilization, the enclosing of the world in a vast electronic web and network of virtual reality and global communication, and the rise of multi-national corporations have set the stage for a new consciousness to emerge. They have set the stage for a new "cup" to emerge that really can hold the steaming hot coffee brewing on the burners of the spiritual worlds. From this point of view, I can understand why the many of our spiritual allies are optimistic.

But even in this optimism, they are not blind to the suffering of humanity, some of that suffering caused by the misuse of the very tools that may make a shift in human awareness possible. They share and partake of that suffering in ways we may never understand from this level of life, keeping the energies of love and vision flowing and not allowing the whole human system to break down in despair. Their efforts are as much about healing and transmutation as about inspiration and stimulation.

Nor are they blind to the world situation and the challenges we face, though they may not see them in quite the same way we do and may in fact see more than we do. What I have been aware of over the years is the number of beings within the subtle worlds working to deal with issues such as the need for new energy sources and ways of ameliorating the worst effects of climate change, or even altering the course of climate change itself, at least within certain parameters set down by physical reality.

This work can take two forms. On the one hand scientists and innovators working in the subtle worlds can make discoveries and develop technologies as much as a their physical counterparts can, and they can attempt to communicate those discoveries to those on earth who can understand and make use of them. On the other hand, the more common methodology is to establish a field of "collaborative energy" and collaborative thought that can enhance the thinking of a physical person, rather like a form of brainstorming between the dimensions. For the most part, for reasons that go beyond the scope of this book, the ideas that will most aid us in the years ahead and shape our future for the better need to come and will come from physical individuals, but this process can be aided by an alliance with similarly concerned and involved beings in the subtle realms. They don't necessarily transmit ideas (though that is always a possibility) but rather enhance the capacity to *have* ideas. They can expand our imaginative thinking, helping us to "think outside the box" and to think and feel in ways that are liberated from the habits and expectations of the past.

The subtle worlds face challenges of inertia and resistance to change within humanity; habits of human action and interaction die hard, and some of those habits would have us go over a cliff rather than find a different path. But the situation is not hopeless. The subtle worlds can't shape our future for us, but they can help shape it with us and give us tools for that shaping when we are open.

Expanding that openness is one of the objectives of the subtle worlds. Knowing the efforts that are being made to further this objective, and knowing the depth of the love and assistance that pours daily from the subtle worlds to us, I cannot help but be optimistic. As I said earlier, from the point of view of the subtle worlds, there is no single future that is inevitable. The future is a landscape of possibilities. Some outcomes are more probable than others, for sure, but these probabilities are always shifting. The future is ours to make, together, not necessarily ours to endure.

Chapter Nine
Consciousness

One of the continuing prophecies of the future over the past fifty years has been that humanity is soon to go through a shift of consciousness that will transform how we think, how we behave, and how we experience reality. We will awaken to abilities to heal ourselves and each other, to heal the ecological wounds of the earth, and to build a utopian civilization. This new consciousness will usher in a golden age.

Expecting a new consciousness to miraculously appear and solve all our problems is a tenuous basket in which to place all our eggs for facing the future. It can lead, as I have experienced in talking with folks who believe deeply in this possibility, to dismissing the challenges we face—and possible ways of addressing them—because the "new consciousness" will take care of all that. It is a more benign version of the apocalyptic view that something outside of us will take care of us because we don't have the ability to do so for ourselves.

The irony for me is that I happen to believe that a new consciousness *is* struggling to emerge in humanity at this time and that this is one of the main areas of focus for helpful and supportive efforts from the subtle worlds. I just don't believe it will happen in the sudden, overnight way that so many of the prophecies describe, nor will it automatically solve anything.

The reason I don't believe in sudden, overnight transformations is simple: it's not the way consciousness works. The real issue isn't change; it's integration and assimilation. As a spiritual teacher, I have seen numerous examples of people suddenly experiencing a metanoia, a spontaneous transformation of their consciousness giving them new insights and understandings, who then lose it because they can't integrate these new insights into their lives. Instant enlightenment can certainly happen, but like winning the lottery, it can cause more problems than it solves if the individual doesn't have a way of holding, integrating, and expressing the new energies that have become part of his or her life. A common result in my observations is not a more balanced and holistic life but ego inflation and disassociation from everyday reality, making the person's incarnation less coherent rather than more so.

In the Seventies, a friend of mine had a dream job working for the Canadian government. At the time, Canada was seeking to boost innovation in the country. My friend headed up an agency that was given a multi-million dollar budget to foster organizations that were researching and applying "new cultural and scientific paradigms" for the advancement and benefit of Canadian society. The criteria for such organizations were very loose, giving him wide latitude in choosing the recipients. Being interested in new forms of spirituality and the vision of the New Age, he decided to use some of his budget to fund some New Age groups in the Toronto area, all of which could legitimately qualify under the terms of his agency's charter. He picked one of the largest and most prominent of these groups and gave them over a hundred thousand dollars in a single grant.

"It was a disaster," he told me later. "Within a couple of months, the group had fallen apart and gone out of business."

"What happened?" I asked.

"They had no infrastructure or decision-making process for handling such a large amount of money. It was more than they could handle. They got into repeated arguments over how to spend what I'd given them, and eventually the conflicts simply shattered the organization. Boy, did I learn a lesson!"

His lesson is the lesson of any sudden influx of new forces whether in the form of money or spiritual insights and subtle energies. Transformation indeed results, but it's not always in a direction we want.

Keeping that in mind, though, it is nevertheless true in my

experience with the subtle worlds that there *is* an ongoing effort to bring a new consciousness to birth within humanity in as integrated a manner as possible. And this effort is accelerating as more and more people are able to respond and begin to integrate the elements of this consciousness into their lives.

I call this consciousness a "Gaian" or "planetary" consciousness, one that enables us to "think like a planet," that is, to think holistically in a manner that creates behavior that benefits all lives on the earth. I think of the planet not simply as a ball of rock spinning through space but as a living presence, Gaia, a "World Soul" that loves, fosters and energizes the unfoldment and evolution of all life on earth, including our own. To think like a planet is to find the capability within ourselves to do the same thing, to be caring towards ourselves, towards each other, and towards the ecology that sustains life on earth.

Giving birth to this consciousness challenges us to shift from a way of life that uses fear, divisiveness and separation to create conditions of wellbeing for only a few to one that uses connection, understanding, relationship, and love to create an emergent wholeness that benefits everyone and everything.

This isn't so much a struggle of good vs. evil, though many might characterize it as such. It's more the struggle against the inertia of bad habits and beliefs to allow a new consciousness, a new way of thinking, feeling, acting and being in the world to take shape. It's the struggle between the habit of a culture of winning, a culture that finds its identity through the defeat, subjugation or elimination of that which is different and which views the "Other" as a threat and danger, and the promise of a culture of partnership that finds its identity in sharing and collaboration and sees the "Other," the stranger and that which is different, as a potential and a resource to be appreciated.

This is not an easy shift to make, for most of us are embedded in the habits of old ways of thinking and doing. It's not just evil corporate oligarchies, greedy bankers, or demented and irresponsible politicians who seek to manipulate the world using fear to create separation and divisions. We all can do it in one way or another, in small ways and large, as we seek to define and protect what is ours.

In *A Paradise Built in Hell*, Rebecca Solnit describes the effect of the beliefs of ordinary people in the aftermath of disasters.

> *In the wake of an earthquake, a bombing, or a major storm, most people are altruistic, urgently engaged in caring for themselves and those around them, strangers and neighbors as well as friends and loved ones. The image of the selfish, panicky, or regressively savage human being in times of disaster has little truth to it. Decades of meticulous sociological research on behavior in disasters, from the bombings of World War II to floods, tornados, earthquakes, and storms across the continent and around the world, have demonstrated this. But belief lags behind, and often the worst behavior in the wake of a calamity is on the part of those who believe that others will behave savagely and that they themselves are taking defensive measures against barbarism.*

She goes on to describe incidents in which innocents were killed by people who felt threatened in this manner even though there were no overt actions taken against them; they simply assumed that people in a disaster will become predators. She concludes this passage saying, "Beliefs matter."

Indeed they do, and beliefs that lead to bad habits of divisiveness and disconnection are not relegated only to the rich, the privileged, or those with political power, though when they are, such individuals can use the power of their positions to enforce those beliefs more devastatingly. We are all potentially culpable, and we are all potentially able to change and express something better. In fact, Solnit's book is an examination of how in the midst of disasters when everything is lost and ordinary life is overturned to the point that survival itself comes into question, people will respond positively by forming connections and relationships that build networks of mutual support and help. If some of the predictions of our future are correct, such disasters may become more and more common, making it more imperative that we understand how people truly respond under such conditions. Perhaps her book should become required reading as preparation for the future.

Divisive and non-holistic ways of thinking and seeing the world are steadily narrowing our options for the future, for they create panic and gridlock at many levels of society in ways that constrain imaginative and creative thinking. They are habits of consciousness that we need to change.

Fortunately, change *is* happening.

At the root of this change is an emerging perspective of what it means to care for the world and for each other, a holistic, ecological, compassionate perspective. It's what I call a "planetary consciousness," as I said, not because it's spread all over the planet but because it's about what it takes to live on and with our planet successfully. This perspective brings with it a whole changing world view based on a convergence of science, systems theory, ecology, spirituality, peace-making, and social justice, all contributing to "skills of wholeness" that can be applied in politics, economics, and in society in general.

But even more important than this holistic world view is the ability to talk with each other across the many divides that past habits have erected between us: racial, ethnic, religious, national, cultural, political, economic, and social divides. Even more important is our ability to connect and to form relationships, for these relationships become the channels along which change can flow.

To do this, we need skills of love; of an imagination that can grasp the value in otherness and difference and can honor and seek out these things; of an awareness of being in partnership with the world, recognizing it's the only home we have and we need to care for it, and a willingness to connect; without these, the most insightful world view, the most profound spiritual teaching, and the most dedicated vision will simply lie inertly in our lives. But a person who is willing to take the steps to form and nurture new connections helps create the arena within which the new world view, the spiritual teaching, and the dedicated vision can live, evolve and act.

I want to be clear about this. The efforts of those beings in the subtle worlds who serve the evolution of humanity and the world as a whole is really not to create a new consciousness, if by this we mean new content to think about or new cosmologies or belief systems. It *is* to enhance the flow of life—physical life and spiritual life—upon the earth. It *is* to enhance the flow of love. It *is* to enhance integration and wholeness. The emergence of a new consciousness is valuable only insofar as it serves and enables the expression of love and the greater manifestation of wholeness. And love and wholeness are not simply ideas; they are actions. They are behaviors. They manifest as connections and relationships born of compassion, caring, honoring, and respect.

The positive signs for our future lie in the fact that more and more people are dedicating themselves to making these connections as well as to embodying and expressing a new, holistic consciousness, a "planetary consciousness." Let's call them *Internauts*.

An Internaut is someone who, whether they know it or not, aids the helpful efforts of subtle worlds by expanding, deepening, and enhancing collaborative relationships. An Internaut can be anyone who is willing to make a connection that wasn't there before, thereby building a pathway along which understanding, imagination, new vision, inspired action, and shared energy may flow. They make collaboration and co-creation possible, even if only in small ways. They may make their connections and form relationships through the Internet and over cell phones—one of the gifts, as I've said, of our civilization's current technological advancement—but not necessarily. They may do their work in town hall meetings, corporate boards, across kitchen tables, and over the back fence. Being an Internaut doesn't mean you use the Internet; it means you explore ways of creating interactions that empower, that heal, that bless, and that serve the emerging wholeness of the world.

We should not underestimate the power of "Internautics." Back in the Seventies, my father was a good friend of a man who spent his life facilitating what in those days was called "citizen diplomacy." He would organize small groups of Americans, usually no more than three or four, to travel to the Soviet Union to meet with equally small groups of Russians; likewise, when possible, ordinary Russians were brought by his organization to the United States to meet and talk with ordinary Americans. These were not high-level diplomatic meetings trying to hammer out policy between the two countries; they were everyday folks from two different cultures building connections between themselves and seeing that "the enemy" was not so different. And these people saw themselves as contributing to a future that was not dominated by mushroom clouds as misunderstanding and hatred led to World War III between the Soviets and the West. They claimed the power to make a difference through relationships, and they did make a difference.

Many peace groups were facilitating this kind of citizen diplomacy in the Seventies and Eighties as a means of building relationships outside the usual political and diplomatic channels along which energies of goodwill and understanding could flow. And even though the Soviet Union has ceased to exist, this movement of ordinary people taking it upon themselves to form connections and relationships to change the world and shape the future continues even more broadly now.   This is the topic of two timely books, *Blessed Unrest* by the social entrepreneur Paul Hawken, and *Global Shift: How a New Worldview is Transforming Humanity*, by psychologist Dr. Edmund Bourne.

Paul Hawken's book is subtitled *"How the Largest Social Movement in History Is Restoring Grace, Justice, and Beauty to the World."* In it he says, "This is the story without apologies of what is going right on this planet, narratives of imagination and conviction, not defeatist accounts about the limits. Wrong is an addictive, repetitive story; Right is where the movement is."

Both of these books talk about a new consciousness emerging on the globe and the way it is spreading through individual or small group connections, often off the radar and unseen by the media. They tell the human, physical story of the love and compassion so evident in the subtle worlds manifesting and taking form in individual lives and the relationships they're forming. They tell the story of "Intranautics" at work.

There are other examples. I have a vivid memory of listening to Phil Lane, Jr., chairman of the Four Worlds International Institute, describing a workshop he gave in Southeast Asia to indigenous tribes about using the Internet for their benefit. He said that young people were coming out of the jungles, having traveled for days on foot or on little motor scooters, to come to this workshop, and all of them were carrying cell phones or some other means of plugging into the Internet. No matter how remote they were, they were wired in to the planetary network, connecting with other indigenous people around the world and planning strategies for helping their various tribes. I was astonished, for I had no idea the Web was that pervasive or could reach into such remote places in the world. But the young people knew about it, appreciated its power and were determined to be connected and part of the wired planet that is evolving.

Another example of Internauts at work is the World Café, founded by Juanita Brown and David Isaacs. The World Café is not a place. It is a process that can happen anywhere, in any place where people come together with a willingness to connect and to converse with each other on topics that matter. Their book, titled *The World Café*, has a subtitle that lays it out: "*Shaping Our Futures Through Conversations That Matter.*"

If we are contemplating a world in which the lights may go out because we can no longer produce cheap electricity or where food is hard to come by or our major coastal cities are underwater due to climate change, we may wonder just what good a conversation may do. But the simple fact is that whatever the nature of our future—whatever finally emerges from the ecology of time—we will survive and prosper in it by knowing and connecting with each other. It will be a collaborative, partnership future, or chances are it won't be a future at all.

The microbiologist Lynn Margulis is a pioneer in endosymbiotic theory which basically says that the eukaryotic cell—the kind of nucleated cell that makes up our body tissue—evolved through a process of symbiosis. As Dr. Margulis has put it, ""Life did not take over the globe by combat, but by networking." In other words, the organisms that survive are those that are most cooperative. Collaboration is at the very foundation of human life; it's literally in our cells.

The challenge before us is to develop the will, the skills, and the knowledge to collaborate more deeply and fully with each other and with the natural world around us. No matter what the future holds, this is essential, and if we do it right, the future may turn out wonderful indeed, far more so than many are expecting right now. The World Café is one "Internautic" step in that direction; it is a process of hosting conversations with people from around the globe that can be the foundation for collaborative relationships. It is overtly a way of developing and nourishing a collective intelligence, something that the subtle worlds can relate to with gusto and even greater collaboration.

A similar step is the work that a friend of mine, Dr. Robert Stilger, is doing to promote what he calls "enspirited leadership" as part of The Berkana Institute. This is an organization dedicated to promoting new forms of collaborative and holistic leadership around the world, particularly with younger people in Third and Fourth World countries. Here is how the Institute describes itself, taken from its website, www.berkana.org:

> *The Berkana Institute works in partnership with a rich diversity of people around the world who strengthen their communities by working with the wisdom and wealth already present in their people, traditions and environment. As pioneers, we do not deny or flee from our global crisis. We respond by moving courageously into the future now, experimenting with many different solutions.*
>
> *Berkana and our partners share the clarity that whatever the problem, community is the answer. We prepare for an unknown future by creating strong and sustainable relationships, by wisely stewarding the earth's resources, and by building resilient communities. We rely on the belief that human beings are caring, generous and want to be together.*
>
> *Each of our initiatives is based on a coherent, in-depth theory of how life organizes in cooperative, generous and interdependent systems — work we've developed with hundreds of colleagues over many years of dialogue, think tanks and*

practical applications in all kinds of settings.

This statement corresponds exactly to the understanding and intentions of the subtle beings with whom I work who are seeking to help humanity. It's about creating relationships which in turn become the foundations for transformation and for shaping the future.

From my perspective, these relationships became channels which subtle beings can use to project love and creative energy from their dimension of consciousness. They are relationships with which they can energetically collaborate and which they can enhance from their level of life. The subtle energies they can add to the process, once we set it into motion through our connections, not only flows into the lives of the individuals directly involved but through them into the energy fields of those with whom they are connected. From the standpoint of the subtle worlds, each of us is an energy rolodex, and if we allow spiritual energies into our lives, the effects can spread to everyone on our energetic address list. Put another way, we are each embedded in an ecology of lives and consciousnesses, and what affects us can spread out into that ecology through the connections we have.

I think of this as a kind of "Gaianplasticity." In modern neuroscience, the most exciting research is in the area of *neuroplasticity*, the power of the brain to change its structure and develop new capacities through the power of our thought and attention. These changes in neural structure have been witnessed and tracked by scientists using methods such as magnetic resonance imaging and nuclear magnetic resonance imaging. There are a number of new books out on this topic; one of the best is *Mindsight*, by Dr. Daniel Siegel. I list others in the Resource section at the back of this book.

There is a similar phenomenon in the subtle worlds. The field of subtle energies around the earth has a similar plasticity to it and is subject to change under the influence of attention, thought, and intention. Connections form in this field much like the neurological connections that form in our brains, only faster and more easily for the most part. Subtle energies of various kinds pass along these connections. The quality and effect of these subtle energies depend on their origin. If they arise from habits of fear and hatred or from a desire to diminish or destroy others who are different from oneself, then they have a toxic effect and will disrupt the capacity of the planet to integrate and become more whole. On the other hand, if the subtle energies come from a consciousness that honors the value of differences and the possibilities that can emerge from them, and from an intentional effort to form connections, then something quite different occurs. An energetic pathway is formed that resonates to the love and presence of Gaia herself and adds to the integration and wholeness of the world. It is these kinds of pathways that endeavors like the World Café and The Berkana Institute are helping to create.

As with any energy system, it's possible that a tipping point may be reached in which the whole collective system of human consciousness does reorganize itself in some manner or opens to a new level of energy and functioning. But if so, it will happen because of the efforts we make now to reconnect humanity to the world and to itself in holistic ways. And because of these efforts, because we will be gaining experience in building and expressing a planetary awareness through our relationships, any new unfoldment of consciousness will arise from who we already are in a manner that we can integrate.

Chapter Ten
Star Power

The other day my oldest son, John-Michael, sent me an email with a link to a website that he thought I would be interested in. "Check this out, Dad," he suggested. It turned out to be a news segment from the TV show *60 Minutes*, and it was about an alternative energy company that after several years of secrecy was finally going public with its new product. The company was Bloom Energy and the product was the BloomBox.

Flash back a few years. I was sitting in the living room of the home of John and Nancy Todd, the founders of the New Alchemy Institute and Ocean Arks International. They are the designers of the bioshelter, at the time a radical innovation combining ecological principles with human architecture to create a house that could generate its own energy without damaging the surrounding environment. The idea of energy independence was very much on their minds, and John and his colleagues had come up with a device that could supply all the electrical needs of the average American home and still have surplus power to feed into a neighborhood grid. This technology was in effect a large transparent water tank containing several layers of fluid at different levels of salinity. As sunlight hit the tank, the chemical interaction between these different layers generated an electrical current.

It looked promising and inexpensive, but the problem was the toxicity of the different salts used in the water to create the layers. Should a tank leak, these salts could pose a biohazard to the surrounding land and to any aquifers under the ground. John decided to scrap the project since he couldn't guarantee that leaks could not or would not occur. But I've always been attracted to the idea that every house could be its own power-plant and a source of energy rather than simple a receiver of it.

Looking at the video and then exploring the company's website, I realized that this is what Bloom Energy is promising with its BloomBox. Using a particular form of a Solid Oxide Fuel Cell made from sand and coated with ink, the company has created a box which can be held in a person's hand and which, they claim, can provide all the electrical needs of a house all day and all night. The fuel cell is non-polluting, clean, and not made from any toxic materials; it does require some energy input to get it going, which is provided by natural gas or other biofuels or even by solar power. Currently, both Google and eBay are using several of the BloomBoxes to power some of their buildings and data farms as an experiment; so far the boxes seem to be performing exactly as the company predicted.

I don't bring this up in order to say that our energy problems are solved or that BloomBoxes will give us the cheap energy we need as a society, though that is the claim Bloom Energy is making. There are problems with the technology still and as with so many of alternative energy technologies, it requires cheap energy (coming from the very fossil fuels that are becoming more expensive) to produce.

Only time will tell if in fact this is a true breakthrough or simply another promise that will fall short of meeting our needs.

The reason I mention this is because it is a model of distributive generation. That is the condition in which a resource is generated at the point of consumption and use rather than at some distant, centralized source. Another example of this is the cell phone. This technology allows the individual to be independent of land lines run by a centralized phone company. When John-Michael moved into a new apartment, he didn't sign up for a phone; he simply uses the cell phone he's had all along. More and more of my friends are getting rid of their land line phones as well in favor of their iPhones and Blackberrys.

Distributive generation gives freedom and independence to the individual or to local neighborhoods and towns; it reduces dependency on centralized systems. Whatever your vision of the future may be, chances are that it will more and more include an emphasis on local development and power. It is entirely possible that either through necessity or through choice and social design, we may agree with economist E. F. Schumacher's vision that "small is beautiful" and shift from large, centralized structures and systems to smaller, more localized ones. John Michael Greer, for instance, does not see any current alternative energy technology such as solar or wind being able to replace fossil fuels for powering the infrastructure of a continental wide civilization as a whole but he definitely sees their use by local communities to meet their more modest energy requirements.

However that may be, I bring it up because it's another way of talking about a shift in consciousness. In the last chapter, I explored the need for a new kind of perceiving and thinking, a new consciousness of ourselves and the world. I spoke of it in terms of connectedness and relationship and the love needed to form those connections. I called it a "Gaian" or "Planetary" consciousness because it is holistic, ecological, and enables us to "think like a planet" in considering how to foster and nourish life and its potentials.

But there is another way of thinking about this emerging consciousness and that is to say that it embodies the principles of distributive generation.

When I wrote about my work with colleagues in the subtle worlds and described their efforts to help humanity at this crucial time in our history, I said that those efforts were directed in two ways. One was towards the cultivation and development of the kind of holistic planetary consciousness I just mentioned and which I discussed in the last chapter. For the spiritual beings involved, the unfoldment and expression of this consciousness is their image of our future, the objective towards which they are working.

The other direction of their efforts is on awakening and nourishing the capacities of the individual. This in effect is an exercise in distributed generation, for in their view, each individual as an energy system is in essence and can be in expression a source of spiritual power and subtle energies.

We do not normally think of ourselves as sources of energy but as recipients. We expect, for instance, to receive blessings from God or spiritual beings, but we may not see ourselves as a source of blessings as well. We expect subtle energies to come from "on high" or from special, "spiritual" people so we may not see ourselves as generative sources of such energies, which can be used to support and nourish the energies of others.

This focus on the spiritual power and resources of the individual—the person as a "spiritual BloomBox"—has been the major focus of my work for the past decade and more; it's basically the work I've taken on in cooperation and collaboration with non-physical allies. I call it "Incarnational Spirituality," for I focus on the processes of incarnation itself as the "engine" that powers our individual spiritual energies.

Metaphorically, the incarnational process is like the sodium oxide fuel cell that powers the BloomBox. This fuel cell operates through the chemical relationship between three layers of material— the anode, the cathode, and electrolyte. In an analogous way, incarnation operates through the relationship between the higher energy state of the soul, the particular state of the personality or the incarnate self, and the world around us. The result of this three-way relationship is the generation of a field of subtle energy and consciousness that we draw upon throughout our physical lives.

This is a very simplistic way to describe the complex system that is a human incarnation. If you want to explore this further, I invite you to visit the Lorian Association website and see the resources for an incarnational spirituality that are there. But I use this simple analogy to suggest why the idea of generative distribution with its implications of individual capacity, power and freedom, is important.

In my classes, I often describe it this way. For millennia we have organized ourselves politically, spiritually, socially, and economically using the metaphor of a sun-satellite system. This postulates the that all energy and power comes from a central source like the sun and is distributed to receivers who, like planets and other satellites, simply reflect and absorb what's given to them. This is true whether the central source is a spiritual being or teacher, a king or emperor, a central bank, a centralized power plant, and so forth.

The shift we need to make in consciousness now is towards a galactic model. A galaxy is filled with stars in relationship with each other. There are dim stars and bright stars, little stars and giant stars, but every star is radiant and generative.

Note that being radiant and generative doesn't mean that you don't also seek out and create relationships as I described in the last chapter; it shouldn't be a conversation-stopper. But it does mean that you have something in yourself that is unique that you can share. John Todd's image of the bioshelter or of his backyard electrical power-generator was not that it only met the energy needs of the house alone; it was designed to generate a surplus that could be fed back into a neighborhood grid. The home thus became independent and interdependent and part of a community.

Many of us go through life wholly unaware of being a generative source or of having a surplus of subtle and spiritual energy. Instead we feel needy and look to outside sources to shine on us and support us. We do need each other to co-create those collaborative fields of energy that can do what no one person can do on his or her own; we do not need to succumb to a habit of neediness. But it takes a shift of consciousness to begin to see oneself as a source, as a living "BloomBox" and not as an otherwise deficient and dependent recipient of energies supplied by others.

But there's more to it than just feeling independent. The field of energy and consciousness that is potentially generated by the incarnational processes is complex and powerful. Most of us only tap and use a very small part of it. Our thinking and imagining is constrained by social and cultural norms, by what others tell us we can do or of what we are capable. We hear about miracles, such as the ones I described earlier or even those that are more dramatic, but we either dismiss them as fantasies or feel they are part of a world that is distant from us: things that happen to other, more special people but never to us.

The fact is that for all our technological progress and prowess as a civilization, we live in great poverty of consciousness. If our civilization does collapse, it may turn out to be a blessing, liberating us to discover the possibilities we really do possess. But maybe we can discover these things without that collapse having to happen or having to happen in overly destructive and apocalyptic ways.

In many ways, the movie *Matrix* captured the mythic import of this consciousness shift. Humanity was essentially asleep, living in a virtual world—the *Matrix*—created by computers. Only a few had escaped and had seen things as they really were. One of these, Neo, discovers how to liberate himself within the *Matrix* and is thus able to express powers within that virtual world that few others can. By demonstrating such powers, he hopes to awaken humanity to the illusion within which it's living and induce a shift of consciousness that will liberate others as well.

Matrix is fiction, and I don't propose that the world is an illusion like the *Matrix*, though there are philosophies that would say that it is. But there is a similar principle at work. We in the materialistic, technological, scientific West have a curiously limited and limiting view of the reality in which we live. For one thing, we generally do not accept that one half of the planet—the non-physical half—even exists and thus cut ourselves off from relationships and partnerships that could be immensely useful, particularly in a time of crisis. That is one reason why the Findhorn Foundation garden developed as it did; like Neo demonstrating his powers of flight to the awed citizens of the *Matrix* in order to awaken them to a larger reality, the Devas told Dorothy Maclean that they were using the miracle of the garden to demonstrate their existence to a materialistic world, and to show what could be done to heal and prosper the earth if there were cooperation with the spiritual forces of Nature.

A friend of mine who is engaged in research into various human potentials says that the field of human nature contains all the possibilities that anyone has ever demonstrated. Thus if a person healed another, potentially any other person could do that. If a person communicates with non-physical beings, then potentially any person can do that. It's all part of the field of possibility.

From my perspective, that field is what is generated by the "fuel cell" of incarnation, and it is vastly underappreciated and underutilized. But throughout history, individuals have demonstrated amazing and phenomenal abilities of consciousness and action which give clues as to just what that field is capable of sustaining and doing. One recent book that I found particularly good in exploring this is *Extraordinary Knowing* by Dr. Elizabeth Lloyd Mayer. Experiencing a kind of miracle event herself, she began an investigation into the science behind such events and their prevalence in society.

Recently a close friend of mine told me about an individual, Mahendra Kumar Travedi, who has been the subject of over four thousand scientific experiments conducted at a variety of universities and laboratories around the world for his documented ability to alter the atomic structure of matter through the power of thought transmissions. He has particularly worked with botanists and others involved in agriculture in experiments in which he generates a field of subtle energy that changes the composition of the soil and energies the growth of plants without any kind of fertilizer being used. The effects he creates are lasting; soil samples taken later after the experiment had ended still showed the chemical differences that he had induced mentally, and the plants continued to grow vigorously even through subsequent generations.

Of course, I cannot substantiate my friend's claims about this individual, but having seen what happened at Findhorn and having witnessed and participated in other miraculous events over the years, it doesn't strain my credulity. As human beings we are far more capable of manipulating and shaping the energy and matter of the physical world than we acknowledge in our current materialistic state of consciousness. Even my father demonstrated this, much to his surprise. A scientist and engineer, he laughed when my mother said that speaking kindly and lovingly to plants and praying over them would make them grow faster and stronger than usual. But she got him to try it out. So he set up an experiment in our house with a variety of plants; he set up control groups in different rooms, and had plants that he prayed over or otherwise spoke in loving and appreciative ways to, plants that he left alone apart from the usual watering and care any gardener would provide (they were his control group), and a third set of plants that he cursed and got angry towards. He ran this experiment faithfully and with scientific vigor for about a month or two, at the end of which he had to admit that Mom was right. The plants that he loved and treated with kindness flourished and indeed grew faster, stronger, and larger than the control group, while the plants he cursed and expressed anger towards were small and sickly and even in some cases died. He became convinced that there was a subtle energy that we generated that could affect the growth and vitality of plants (and years later, though after I had left, he and Mom moved to Findhorn for a few years).

My friend Lee Irwin whom I wrote about earlier is one of the leading scholars in the United States in Native American spirituality and, being part Native American himself, has been allowed to participate in a number of spiritual ceremonies. Over the years, he has seen medicine people do amazing things with healing and the manipulation of subtle energies; he has experienced some of these phenomena himself, as in the healing of his student. In this regard, the Native American author Vine Deloria wrote a book remembering the powers of the ancestral medicine men, *The World We Used To Live In*.

Another friend, John Perkins, has spent years studying and working with the shamans of the Amazon rain forest and has also seen miracles performed that defy the known laws of science. Indeed, for these shamans, the future exists not in time but in our dreams, by which they mean not simply the experiences we have at night when we're sleeping but our paradigms, our worldview, our understanding of reality, and the way we imagine ourselves and the world—in effect, the overall state and shape of our consciousness. We are manifesting our dreams. If our dreams are violent, disconnected and destructive, that is the form our future will take. Their message to Westerners is consistent: change your dreams if you want to change the future.

In short, each individual comes into life with amazing abilities to relate to and interact with the world in ways that our culture would call miraculous. That we don't all express these capacities is because we don't tap into the full potential of our incarnational field of consciousness and energy; there are different reasons for that, the most influential being that the larger cultural field of consciousness—the worldview of consensual reality—denies these capacities are there and is more oriented to creating a sun-satellite system of organization than it is in empowering a galactic, star-filled one. Though our culture pays lip-service to individual achievement and freedom, it is careful to place boundaries and limits on just what those achievements can be and how much freedom a person can truly have. Our culture, like so many before it, values centralization.

But perhaps the threats of the future will put pressure on us to allow new modes of consciousness and capacity to awaken and express. If the energy crisis of the 21st century can foster new models of distributive generation such as BloomBoxes, perhaps the consciousness crisis will enable us to rediscover our star power and bring our incarnational capacities to bloom as well.

Chapter Eleven
Facing the Future

What prompted me to write this book was the question that I'm asked as a spiritual teacher: how do we face the future? What steps can we take to prepare for or to shape our tomorrows? In this and the next chapter, I want to summarize my answer, drawing on the ideas I've been discussing. At least, it's my answer now based on the information, insights, and understanding I currently have. It could change in the....well, in the future!

Let's take stock of where we are. When people have asked me about the future, it is almost always in conjunction with some negative or apocalyptic prophecy or in regard to what they perceive as pessimistic images of a dark future. If they believe the future is going to be more of the same of what we already have, only better, or if they are sure Utopia is on our doorstep, they don't ask me about it. Why should they? For them, the future's not a problem.

As I've said in different ways throughout this book, I feel the future is unfolding, and a variety of elements are contributing to that unfoldment. No one can say with absolute certainty that this is what the future will be like. Miracles can turn the darkest prophecies around and present us with something unexpected and wonderful; by the same token, overconfidence and complacency or just plain bad planning and mistakes can turn a positive momentum into a slide down into disaster.

Trying to predict and navigate the future can be a bit like playing *Chutes and Ladders*!

But keeping that in mind, there are four main contenders for tomorrow-hood that are confronting us right now. When people ask me how to face the future, it's one or more of these four that they're usually thinking of. I portray them in the following chart along with some of the suggestions I've seen people make by way of response.

Note that I do not include Apocalypse of any kind as one of the four possibilities, although the worst consequences of any of these four could be considered apocalyptic. This is because I do not consider an apocalypse as a possible future. There is no one singular planetary event coming up that will destroy everything and kill everyone except a chosen few who will build a new utopian civilization. Although my contacts and colleagues in the subtle realms have said that we are at a threshold moment, a critical time, in human history, they have never said there will be an apocalyptic event; indeed, for the past fifty years they have been consistently adamant that such an event is not going to happen and will not happen. As my friend and mentor John once said somewhat wryly, "Humanity is not going to get off that easily, with everyone flooding into the subtle worlds where things seem safe and easy and then letting the gods make everything right again. It's your responsibility; you need to fix the problems on earth you've created and learn wisdom in the process."

This does not mean, however, that there are no disasters in our future. Ask the citizens of New Orleans about that or most recently, the citizens of Haiti. Again, John did prophesy that there would be "mini-apocalypses" affecting localized areas but having wide ripple effects throughout all of humanity. But disasters like that have been happening throughout our history. If we're more vulnerable to them now, it's because there's a larger human population, and much of it is living in areas that are vulnerable areas anyway. When the second largest city in the United States sits on top of one of the most active and destructive earthquake faults in the country, one doesn't need to be a prophet to know that there's a heightened potential for disaster.

Note as well that the four futures listed are actually *current* conditions which are producing consequences. They are the seeds right now for four possible consequential futures. In this way, it isn't so much the future that we need to face but the present.

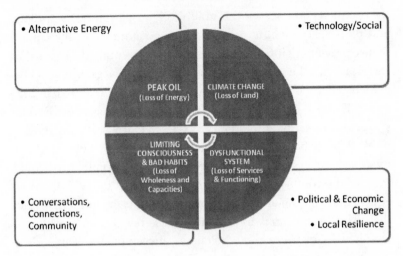

FIGURE 1: Four Possible Consequential Futures
and Four Responses

In Figure 1, we see a circle divided into four quadrants, and each quadrant lists a current condition and its potential consequences.

- Peak Oil threatens us with a loss of the cheap energy on which our civilization has come to depend, causing economic consequences and a potential breakdown of services and technologies that require cheap fossil fuels. One of the areas hard hit could be food production since so much of it uses fertilizers that are made from petroleum products, not to mention the gasoline used for tractors and other farm machinery or to transport food products to markets around the world.

- Climate Change threatens us with a loss of land due to the rising of sea levels and the desertification of other areas as temperatures get hotter. This is the big one, for the consequences here could be more devastating to all life on earth through the disruption of various ecosystems than the effects of peak oil, which are mainly restricted to human societies.

- Dysfunctional System means that the institutions and systems of our civilization are no longer able to operate properly and serve the common good. We see this graphically displayed in the gridlock and partisanship that is paralyzing the government of the United States, preventing it from making and implementing decisions that can deal with the many problems the country faces. But it is also evident in the global economic system which nearly collapsed in 2008 and 2009 and as of this writing is still not out of the woods as Europe struggles to deal with the debts of Greece that were being hidden by Wall Street banks. Nor can religion be let off the hook here as a dysfunctional system. Fanatical beliefs of varying faiths are behind most of the conflicts and terrorism in the world today without an equivalently strong and vital effort by religious institutions within the different traditions to challenge these beliefs and work more strenuously for peace and wholeness between human beings. The result of the dysfunctions in the major systems of society is a loss of effective service and capabilities that truly contribute to the good of the whole.

• I wrote about limiting consciousness and bad habits of belief and action in the last chapter. Whether it's an overly materialistic worldview, a limited view of human capacities, a belief in humanity against nature or one part of humanity against another, or the habits of division and separation, the end result is that a loss of personal and collective wholeness and a concomitant loss of important human capacities that emerge when there is love, connection, and collaboration.

The circular arrows in the middle of the circle indicate that in reality these conditions and challenges are not isolated from each other. Instead they feed into and magnify each other. We've had dysfunctional political and economic situations in the past, but now the negative consequences are magnified by the fact that the implications and results of peak oil and climate change are adding to the pressures on government, the economy, and other sectors of society, making everything much more complex and dangerous than it might be otherwise. Factor in a consciousness intent on winning at all costs and unwilling to compromise or cooperate, and you have a much more critical and potentially disastrous situation than might be here otherwise if all our leaders were acting collaboratively for the good of the whole.

For each of these four conditions, I have listed in a box just outside the circle, one or two of the responses that I've seen in the literature.

- For Peak Oil, the usual response is some form of alternative energy that can either replace petrochemicals or take up the slack as fossil fuels become more expensive and less available. The challenge to this is three-fold. The first is that there is no alternative energy that can match the concentrated energy that is in petroleum. Fossil fuels are extremely concentrated forms of solar energy created over millions of years under special geological conditions. No other energy source comes close to possessing the same "bang for the buck." The second problem is that it takes energy to get energy. At the moment, all alternative energy technologies require an expenditure (in some cases a very high expenditure) of fossil fuel energy to produce; this is because most of the alternatives being proposed actually represent a high level of technological sophistication.

This is the problem, for instance, with turning corn into ethanol as a gasoline substitute. It costs more energy to produce the ethanol than is saved by using ethanol in an automobile or truck (not to mention the loss of food corn as acreage is planted in corn destined to become fuel).

The third challenge is that our energy infrastructure is built around petroleum. Even as new technologies are developed, it costs money and energy to adapt them to the existing energy grid or distribution networks or to build entirely new ones. The cost of adaptation in terms of money and energy may be more than the new technology can pay back. (The BloomBox, by using distributive generation which bypasses the normal electrical grid, is one strategy for doing an end run around this particular problem.)

The fact is that a very cheap and highly concentrated form of energy is running out because like all things on this earth, it's finite in its supply. This is a fact of nature to which we need to adapt.

- Technology is also the usual response to climate change, along with social innovations. These include ways of protecting coastal cities, of sequestering carbon emissions, of implementing strategies of conservation, and of finding ways of dealing with waves of immigration as people leave areas that are being rendered barren or unlivable due to rising temperatures or rising sea levels.

- For the dysfunction of our political and economic systems, there are attempts to implement institutional change, but so far they have not been terribly successful. Old habits die hard, and as I mentioned above, the culture of winning holds a powerful sway over peoples' imagination and intentions. There is more hope at local levels where grassroots organizations and neighborhood communities can begin to work out ways of dealing with peoples' everyday needs. Should the national government and economy collapse, which is always a possibility when there is systemic dysfunction—the economy, after all, came very close to it in 2008 by all accounts—it will be the local governments that will pick up the pieces, so this is where the most creative work can be done and is being done.

- The New Age movement in the late Sixties and all through the Seventies was one strategy for promoting a new worldview and seeking to bring a more holistic, planetary consciousness to birth. In some ways, it still is at least to the extent that it provides an arena still for people to explore expanded human capacities. There is a growing body of research as well into such capacities which, at least for those involved, opens windows on new possibilities and new vistas of consciousness. But the main engines for consciousness change, it seems to me, are the many movements simply encouraging people to talk together and explore their differences and give birth to new ways of seeing the world. The work is being done through all the grassroots organizations that are implementing connections around the world, facilitated and mediated by the Internet and other technological tools of communication.

So here are the current conditions and their consequent futures that we are facing, and here are a few of the responses that seek to turn the lemons of the present into lemonade in our tomorrows. This is hardly an exhaustive list. The books I list in the Resources section are also just a tip of the iceberg of the literature that's available in books, periodicals, articles, websites, videos and so on dealing with our possible futures and how to face them. But hopefully if you're interested, they will give a place to start your own explorations.

But looking at Figure 1, there is for me something missing. It's a key ingredient. It's as if we're looking at a complex Bach piano concerto and trying to play it with one hand. It won't be successful; something crucial will be left out.

Einstein famously said that "We cannot solve our problems with the same thinking we used when we created them." This is part of what's missing as well. We're looking at the future—at the problems of the present—through the same consciousness that is creating them. We need something different. We need different thinking.

So here is my bias. I don't believe we have a chance of dealing successfully with the problems currently before us or ahead of us without partnering with our allies in the subtle worlds. They are our other hand in playing the concerto, and we need to expand our thinking and our awareness to embrace the reality as well as the potentials they represent.

Of course, religious traditions have accepted and dealt with the reality of non-physical beings for millennia, but for me, they are not solely or purely religious figures. As I describe in my book *Subtle Worlds*, I have a more naturalist viewpoint of them, for I have experienced them as fellow living beings dwelling in their own ecologies and for the most part sharing with me a love for this planet. They are the members of earth's other half, its "second ecology," and many of them are as concerned as we are for humanity's overall wellbeing and success and the emergence of a true planetary culture that can express in physical ways the wholeness that exists in spirit. While I respect and honor the various religious traditions and their views of these beings—and the centuries of wisdom they have accumulated in dealing with them—I feel it's time to liberate them from a purely religious framework and see them in a broader perspective as our partners in the life of Gaia.

So when I read the various books about the future, whether about peak oil and its consequences or global climate change or books on new technologies and strategies for dealing with these problems, such as Stewart Brand's excellent new book *Whole Earth Discipline: An Ecopragmatist Manifesto,* I come away feeling incomplete and thinking, "but yet...what about....?" None of these books even begins to deal with the presence and influence of the subtle worlds, which is hardly surprising given that they are not considered part of "real reality" in our culture. Even an excellent book on the spiritual side of peak oil and the decline of industrial culture, Carolyn Baker's *Sacred Demise: Walking the Spiritual Path of Industrial Civilization's Collapse* approaches the spiritual dimension as a means of coping and dealing with grief and despair. This is important to be sure, but it's not the same as exploring how that dimension as a real force in our lives can participate in change and co-creation or how it can be a partner in shaping the future.

Again, I'm not surprised by this; we are facing serious issues in the material world, and it's only natural that the discussion of these issues and possible solutions is focused in a material way, dealing only with the physical and psychological side of things. What can a non-physical being do, after all, about excess greenhouse gases in the atmosphere or diminishing reserves of petroleum and natural gas? What can a non-physical being do about anything in a physical universe? Why waste time and energy—and our credulity—even discussing it?

But the fact is, as human history abundantly demonstrates, the subtle worlds and non-physical beings can affect, have affected, and in all probability will continue to affect physical events and situations. This is where the tradition of miracles has come from. Furthermore, as a human being taps into his own expanded incarnational field—his generative "star" field, to use the metaphor from the last chapter—he can work wonders and miracles as well. I've seen it happen, and I've even made it happen (though not nearly as much as I would like—I have a great deal still to learn). It happened at Findhorn. It's happened many times with my friend Lee Irwin, and it happened in the healing of my other friend dying of cancer. It's why I wrote about miracles in this book and said that a consciousness of miracles is necessary in dealing with the challenges before us and creating a positive future.

Miracle is a tricky word, as I said earlier. For most people it means either something supernatural –a suspension of natural law—or a last hope when all other possibilities are gone. "The only thing that can save us is a miracle," and such a statement borders on wishful thinking—and depending on the context may in fact be wishful thinking.

But that is not how I'm using the term. A miracle to me is an application of a natural law but one based on relationship and requiring the participation of multiple levels of consciousness and energy. A miracle is nothing more, really, than a fulfillment of Einstein's statement, an application of thinking and acting on a level different from the one that created the problem in the first place. A miracle suspends nothing; rather it expands. It adds to. It heightens. It broadens the consciousness and the energy involved so that a "different level" can be brought into play than the one that created the problem.

When my wife and I sit together and talk over an issue and come to insights we wouldn't have come to on our own because we have been inspired by our relationship and the energy we share, this is a miracle. It's a common one, an everyday one, but it fulfills my definition above. Her consciousness and mine have come together and been able to communicate, facilitated by a relationship vibrant with love and mutual respect, hence providing multiple levels of consciousness and energy.

When Juanita Brown and David Isaacs convene a World Café and get strangers involved in conversations that give birth to new connections, new insights, new consciousness and new solutions to old problems, they are working a miracle. Not because it's extraordinary, not because it suspends natural law or goes against expectations, but because it fulfills the potential of those relationships and connections; it adds to them, it expands them into a field of possibility and thought one might not reach on his or her own.

Miracle is another word for what can happen in a co-creative partnership when the dynamics of that partnership create a field of thought and mutual feeling that can transcend the limitations of the moment and open the door to possibilities and potentials. To work miracles is the innate power of the human being through our capacities to love, to form connections, to create wholeness, and to allow for emergence, for something new to unfold. We truly are miracle-workers; that is part of our "star power."

Working with the subtle worlds is another kind of partnership, a kind of meta-world café. It brings certain advantages and, yes, disadvantages, which I describe in Subtle Worlds and other writings. Subtle beings can bring a fresh and different perspective, one that can be very helpful in sorting out paths to follow. They can offer guidance and advice, often through dreams, which can also be very helpful, though I believe this is the least important thing that they can offer, in part because their perspective doesn't always lend itself to an understanding of the physical world so their advice can at times be confusing or not very useful. In my experience, the most powerful thing they offer is a collaboration of energy that has the effect of giving a person greater access to his or her own expanded field of consciousness. In short, they help us go to a different level of thinking than the one that created the problem. This can be invaluable. They can facilitate connections and enhance our capacity to love and to create wholeness. We still have to hold the intention and do the work, but they can multiply the effects.

But can they reverse global warming, for instance? Can they help us in big, planetary ways like that? I don't know; the Devas at Findhorn told Dorothy that the miracle of the garden was only a small sample of what could be done. The land, the air, and the water could all be cleansed of pollution, they said, if human beings could cooperate with them. But that's a big "if."

However, in an important way, this question misses the point. The subtle worlds are not a new "technology" that we can use to make the world the way we want it to be. It's not like they're there to serve our desires and make sure we're not discomfited or inconvenienced. They are there to help us fulfill our destiny of becoming (among other things) a true and loving partner with Gaia. This means truly learning to think like a planet, which means to think in terms of the good of the whole as well as the good of the part. Global warming is certainly a threat to us, but at the moment we're a threat to just about every other life form on earth. We are in the midst of a human-caused mass extinction event of a magnitude the earth has not seen for millions of years; a lot of species of living beings are disappearing forever because we want to have a particular lifestyle. Working with the Devas and other angelic intelligences within nature means at least gaining some perspective on the needs of the whole. If I ask the subtle worlds to reduce the rain in Seattle, might that rain show up someplace else that is not prepared for it? What might get flooded so I can have more sunny days? If we are learning any lessons at all these days, it's how to live in a complex, dynamical, interdependent and interrelated system, something the subtle worlds actually know quite a lot about.

I actually think, if they wished, that the subtle worlds could reverse the worst conditions of the pollution causing climate change; they do have that power. But again, it's not magic. It would require an immense amount of subtle energy to shift the patterns so dramatically. Where does that subtle energy come from? Much of it would have to come from us, generated by our love and our capacity to form the necessary connections and wholeness that could let that kind of power flow where needed. Otherwise, there is the risk of creating more imbalance, more dis-integration, more incoherency. The planetary system has to shift as a whole, not just in parts, and for that to happen, we need to be part of that whole in intent, in consciousness, and in our behavior. That is what is meant by "cooperating with the Devas."

As I said, they're not magical, only miraculous! By this I mean that they work in harmony with natural law, not against it. The garden at Findhorn represented an augmentation of the natural forces of life and growth in the soil and in the plants, a process that apparently Trivedi uses when he changes soil vitality and composition by the use of his thoughts alone. Miracles work because of nature, not against it. Perhaps an archangel or some suitably advanced being could suspend or change the laws of thermodynamics—the knowledge of whether it could or not is way above my pay grade—but I doubt it.

It isn't the way they work, in my experience.

Can they restore the oil we've burnt so profligately over the past hundred years or so in order to reverse Peak Oil? Only in our dreams. Some of our consequences we are going to have to live with, but what the subtle worlds can do is help us live with them more gracefully in ways we may not expect or know how to do on our own.

The subtle worlds cannot make our problems go away—at least not most of them or the big ones—but they can help us achieve a level of energy and consciousness where we can see those problems differently and develop solutions that may escape us now. They can enhance our potentials, our capabilities, our insights, but we still have to do the work. We still have to make the changes that a new consciousness will require. Perhaps most importantly, they can help us become part of the planetary whole in ways that can permit balanced, integrated and coherent changes and shifts to take place.

So let's look at our diagram again but this time adding partnership with the subtle worlds to the mix.

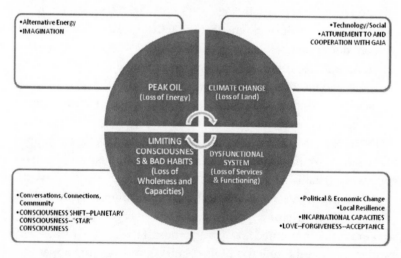

FIGURE 2: Adding the Missing Ingredient
Partnership with the Subtle Worlds

Figure 2 is the same as Figure 1 except now some additional items have been added to the response boxes. These represent some of what can be added when we incorporate partnership with the subtle worlds into our thinking about the future.

• In conjunction with Peak Oil, the subtle worlds can enhance the power of imagination. Basically, they can help us think outside the box, in part through the energy collaboration I mentioned that enables us to expand our thinking and go to that "different level" to which Einstein referred. One good example of this for me is Stewart Brand in his new book *Whole Earth Discipline*. Stewart has been an environmentalist for longer than I have known him, right back to when he started the *Whole Earth Catalog*. But in this book he thinks outside his own box in imaginative ways, drawing upon nuclear power, genetic engineering, and other disciplines to come up with some innovative ways of dealing with the deteriorating environmental situation in the world. The issue for me in this case is not whether all of his ideas will work—there are legitimate pros and cons about the use of nuclear energy, for instance—but he is using his imagination to open new possibilities and to think in ways one might not expect him to. He has a positive view of the future and of our capacity to partner with the earth in making a beautiful and practical culture come into being.

Imagination is too often belittled in our culture for we equate it with fantasy and an escape from reality. But, as Robert Moss eloquently testifies in his book *The Three Only Things*, imagination is one of the most powerful tools we have to go beyond the known, to contact the subtle worlds, and even more importantly, to make connections with each other.

Peak Oil demands that we rethink just about every aspect of our civilization, either to find ways to keep a high level of technology and energy or to adjust in graceful ways to a lower level of the same. This requires us to use imagination. The status quo is gone or going; the near-depression of 2008 and 2009 dramatically showed us that we can't do business as usual. It's our imagination that will help us shift from the familiar into new territory.

And it is imagination that may see in the world a new relationship or process in physics or chemistry, something no one has yet seen or thought of, but which will so revolutionize our understanding that whole new kinds of technologies, perhaps even psychic ones, will emerge. Peak Oil doesn't mean the end to exploring or to learning; it doesn't mean the end of innovation and discovery, unless we give up our imaginations and our capacity to think outside the box and to be spacious in our thinking.

I consider imagination to be the ability to form new connections, to think in new channels and in new ways, and to perceive what no one else is seeing. But like the subtle worlds themselves, it cannot do magic. Had Leonardo da Vinci imagined an internal combustion engine, he still could not have manufactured one nor powered it, for the technology to do so didn't exist in his time nor did the gasoline. Imagination cannot produce what isn't there. If an invention requires a resource that is no longer available, imagination will not make up the deficit. Nor can it arbitrarily change the laws of physics and chemistry which create limits in the natural world; science fiction is filled with examples of wonderful technologies that could not exist according to the laws of nature as we now know them but which work perfectly in the pages of fiction.

But then, that's the kicker: "the laws of nature as we know them." If there are other laws, other principles, other insights out there beyond the boundaries we've explored, it's the imagination— the capacity to think broadly and deeply in new ways and to form new connections with the world—that will open the door to them.

• With climate change, opening to the subtle worlds brings attunement to and partnership with Gaia and with the intelligences and forces of nature. Can this stop global warming? This depends, as I said earlier, on how deeply and well we can integrate ourselves with the integral wholeness of the planet. How effectively and deeply can we as a species hold planetary energies and the life-field of Gaia? Deeply and effectively enough to change the weather and the atmosphere and other homeostatic systems at work in global warming? Maybe. The atmosphere is an information system the same as any other, and Angels and Devas can change that information if it doesn't violate larger principles of natural law or introduce incoherency into the larger system of the planet by damaging some other part of the earth.

But if Findhorn is any example, local effects could definitely be obtained, ameliorating some of the worst effects of rising temperatures, though if new sea levels are flooding New York City, I doubt there's anything the subtle worlds could do about it. To refreeze the Arctic icepacks, assuming it even could be done by the Devas and nature spirits, would require an immense amount of energy and systemic integration to preserve the wholeness of the entire system. Again, cooperation with these beings doesn't work magic; it works along established organic and energetic pathways, not against them. This cooperation can create new channels of possibility, but these channels are still within the organic integrity of the planetary system as a whole. There are limits to what even Angels and Devas can do, but within those limits is a great deal of room for co-creation and change.

The important point to grasp here is that those beings who seek to partner with us, the Angelic and Deva consciousnesses, for instance, as well as the wise ancestors and teachers of our species, do have an innate feel for the integration and wholeness of things, often in ways we lack. What we have is an innate feel for the particularity and individuality of things. To use a crude and much overworked analogy from quantum physics, we are aware of the particle while the subtle worlds are aware of the wave. We really do have knowledge and insights about this world that those on the subtle worlds need and cannot readily gain on their own. The same is true in reverse.

This is why partnership is so important. We know how to fit the little pieces together, but they know how those pieces are part of a larger whole. We may not know how a particular action, such a constructing a building in a particular site or damming a river, may affect a larger environmental or energetic whole, but there are beings in the subtle worlds who do and can help us to these things in a more integrated fashion.

• When institutions begin to become dysfunctional and break down, the individual is more often than not thrown back on himself or herself, left to his or her own resources. Bringing the subtle worlds into the picture can greatly enhance and extend those resources, at least in terms of inner capacities. This can happen in two ways. On the one hand, capacities for healing, blessing, manifestation, and the like become more available as the individual's own incarnational field is enhanced through energetic partnership with the subtle worlds. When Lee healed his student, he used capacities innate in each of us; in effect, they saved the student when medical science said it was hopeless. If we find that the medical services we've become used to in our culture become less available or too expensive, or the system just breaks down, being able to heal each other will be a handy skill indeed.

The second benefit is that when we have access to our own expanded field—when our hearts open in love and forgiveness to one another and in willing acceptance of each other, we become able to create new, healthier systems to replace the ones that are breaking down and becoming dysfunctional. This is the kind of dynamic that Rebecca Solnit describes so eloquently and well in her book *A Paradise Built in Hell*.

• Finally, recognizing, understanding and working with the subtle worlds is both part of and contributes to a shift of consciousness for individuals and for humanity as a whole. To find we have a partnership with beings who truly wish us well and can add their energies to ours in synthesis and synergy, enhancing our capacities, can give us hope. It can also give us a new look at ourselves, allowing us to see ourselves as worthy, valuable, loved members of the Gaian community of life. The subtle worlds can most definitely help in establishing both a Gaian or Planetary Consciousness and an incarnational or "Star" consciousness.

This only scratches the surface of this topic. I am not trying to give an exhaustive list of all the things that could be done in partnership with the subtle worlds. That would be impossible, in part because some of the possibilities would be emergent, not known either to us or to them until they actually manifested in relationship to a particular situation. That's the thing about collaborative fields: they make emergent phenomena possible, things which cannot be predicted ahead of time.

All I want to do is to suggest possibilities. Working with the subtle worlds is a skill and a discipline all its own, but it's one that can be learned and developed. I've been teaching it to people for some time now, though I also am learning. The focus for me is not on getting "messages" or information, guidance or advice, but on a partnership of living and loving energy that introduces spaciousness into the human system and opens up what I metaphorically think of as our "star" consciousness, the larger field of our incarnational wholeness and capacities.

The fact is that I don't think we can fully understand, prepare for, or shape our future without taking into account our own expanded capacities and the existence of and potential relationship with the subtle worlds. In so doing, we can expect miracles—though not magic. Our culture is based on very large systems—big government, big business, big agriculture, big everything--and the cheap energy that powers them. This largeness gives us efficiencies in economies of scale but it can also disempower individuals in ways that work against human evolution and wellbeing. There is a real question as to whether our civilization should survive. Is it really the best we can create? Can we not do better?

I know that our partners and potential partners in the subtle worlds are seeking ways to accomplish transformation that do not entail the suffering or deaths of millions or even billions of people. Is that going to be possible? I don't know. I only know that the effort is being put forth in the spiritual worlds to make it possible, and many people in the physical world are responding. In the end, it will depend on us as always, for this is our world and we are responsible.

But the world we know and see every day is also only half a world. When it comes to facing the future, coming into partnership with its other half is more than half the battle.

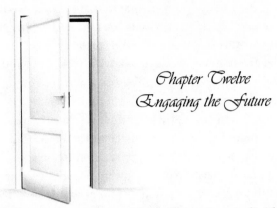

Chapter Twelve
Engaging the Future

How anyone engages with the future is an individual matter. It depends on who you are and your life circumstances. It depends on what your vision of the future is or what kind of future you want to see manifest. Where you live and the culture that surrounds you makes a difference. If you feel that being part of a supportive community is an important strategy for your future, whether it's an actual residential one or a network of friends and neighbors, how readily and easily does the culture and society around you support this? Whether you live in a rural, an urban or a suburban setting can affect such a strategy as well. When I was working as an adjunct professor for the University of Wisconsin, one of the projects in which I was engaged because of my prior Findhorn experience was to help create an intentional community. People were willing but often lacking in community skills as they came from very individualistic, urban backgrounds where they were more used to living autonomously. I used to joke that we might need to recruit a team from a Third World country to teach the First Worlders how to live together.

So I cannot tell you how to prepare for the future. Only you can determine that for yourself. But I can offer some suggestions and share some steps and some thoughts that may help.

First, and I believe most importantly, is not to fear the future. Fear constricts our ability to think deeply and broadly; it restricts our imagination and our creativity. It constrains our energy and may keep us in habitual ways of reacting, which may themselves be part of the problem.

When I feel afraid, I find someone to share my fears with and talk them out. Usually this is my wife, but it could be any trusted friend or even a counselor, someone who can listen objectively and with empathy. If you have no one to talk with, then write your fears down. Getting your fears out into the open and looking at them relieves a lot of the pressure.

When I talk out my fears, I always discover they fall into at least two categories: those I can do something about and those I can't. For the former, I take whatever actions or precautions seem appropriate. For instance, we have a very old maple tree that stands over our house. For some months, whenever there was a fierce windstorm, I would become worried that a large limb or even the tree itself might fall and damage the roof of the house. I talked about it with Julia, and we brought in a professional to evaluate the health of the tree. As it turned out, there were problems, and we were able to take protective measures (which happily did not involve cutting the tree down).

For those fears that are more abstract or that I can't do anything about directly, I simply acknowledge them and then get on with my life. I find the best antidote to that kind of fear is to be busy contributing something by being active in the world.

I also have complete trust that I will be in the place and with the people that is best for me and for others. This trust comes in part from my work with the subtle worlds and my knowledge of the protection and help that is extended to each of us if we are open to receive it intuitively, through dreams, or in some other way. Trust is an important strategy in dissolving fear, for if I give in to my fears, I may take actions that make the situation worse rather than better.

In the summer of 1982 I read an article in the newspaper about a family in Canada who had become convinced that World War III was going to break out and that North America would be the target of numerous nuclear bombs. They were sure the Northern Hemisphere would become inhospitable for years due to fallout, so they went to what they believed was be the safest place they could find where war wouldn't touch them. They moved to the Falkland Islands off the coast of Argentina. They had been there two weeks when the Argentinean army and navy invaded the island, leading to the Falkland war with Great Britain. Their home was in the middle of the fighting.

Sometimes when we try to run from our fears, we end up in the place where they are realized, and at other times when we trust our intuition, we end up in a safe place. I know that at times it can be hard to distinguish one from the other; this comes with experience. But I take a large step in discernment if I can find ways to diminish my fears and not let fearful emotions impulsively dictate my actions.

The first rule for me, then, is simply this: don't engage the future with fear.

One thing that helps in dealing with fear is knowledge. I find it's helpful to get as much information and as wide a picture of the possibilities before us as I can. That's why I read both Peak Oil blogs and anti-Peak Oil blogs, for instance. That's why I would read John Michael Greer and Stewart Brand, or listen to the high-tech people who say technology will save us and the low-tech people who say it won't. No one, however wise, has the whole picture. We each see the world and the future from our own points of view. Granted, some of these points of view are better informed and come from a richer base of experience and critical thinking than others, so you want to be discerning in whom you pick to study. There are a lot of people in the world who are simply transmitting their fears or making sensational claims for reasons that have little to do with your welfare or with actually creating a better future. The Internet in particular is open to all comers and is notorious for the misinformation it contains. Yes, you can find diamonds in the rough by surfing the web, but you find an awful lot of rough, too.

In the end, you will have to make up your mind about the future, but in the process, keep an open mind and keep it as well informed as you can. It may help to remember that the future is basically a hypothesis that hasn't been proven yet. We are testing that hypothesis in the creativity and activity of our lives. The important quality of a hypothesis is not that it isn't true but that it's open to falsification or verification as new data comes in. Keep open to that flow of information.

At the same time, act on whatever hypothetical future you choose.

Be practical and smart. If you feel that there may be food shortages in the future, learn to grow a garden. Learn about permaculture, for instance. If you feel the Peak Oil literature describes the future that is ahead of us, then educate yourself in steps you can take in your community to prepare. A place to start could be in learning about the Transition Town movement. This is a grassroots movement that asks and attempts to answer the following "Big Question" which I have taken from their website, www.transitiontowns.org.:

> For all those aspects of life that this community needs in order to sustain itself and thrive, how do we significantly increase resilience (to mitigate the effects of Peak Oil) and drastically reduce carbon emissions (to mitigate the effects of Climate Change)?

Shaun Chamberlin and Rob Hopkins have excellent books on this topic which I list in the Resources section of this book. Likewise, David Holmgren's book, *Future Scenarios: How Communities Can Adapt to Peak Oil and Climate Change*, provides a more general look; he also has an excellent book out on Permaculture.

Whatever you do, to go back to our first rule, you should do without fear. Your practical actions should be directed creatively to building a positive future within whatever limits and probabilities you decide are logical and warranted. Don't become involved in a transition town community because you think it's the best way to survive in a post-industrial world, but because you think it has qualities and potentials that would make for a good future, and you want to support and build them. In other words, act positively and proactively, not in reaction or fear. You will have more success with whatever steps you take if you do so. And as far as the subtle worlds go, they can enter into a collaborative energy partnership—blending their energy with ours in generating a creative field of thought and vision—more easily and powerfully if we are moving ahead with positive emotions and energies than if we are acting in fearful ways.

However, I would also suggest exploring other possible futures as well and not putting all your eggs in one basket. This falls under the category of being open to a wide range of information and insights, including data that suggests your original hypothesis of the future may need to be modified in some way. But it has another purpose as well which falls into the category of subtle energy flow.

Studies in neuroplasticity have demonstrated that our attention and intentions can direct brain activity in such a way that new connections are formed and the brain structure alters in favor of the activity or direction of that attention. A similar condition exists in the subtle worlds, a kind of "Gaianplasticity," as I have already mentioned. The force of our thoughts and emotions, our attention and intention can manifest pathways of energy along which subtle forces flow as well, changing probabilities as they do.

For example, I can accept that we are running out of cheap energy from fossil fuels—in a finite world, that is a given, not a speculation, and nearly all the current data suggests that we have either passed the peak in world oil production or will do so in the next two or three years—thereby accepting that a deconstruction of industrial society due to the increasing cost and decreasing availability of fossil fuels is likely to happen. I can make that my hypothesis of the future and take actions accordingly as I mentioned above. In so doing, I add to the currents of subtle energies already gathering around the thought-forms involved with Peak Oil and its consequences. It's as if I were a grant making foundation, and I pledged all my money and resources to the Peak Oil movement.

But now, to continue this metaphor, along comes a young scientist who says, "If I had some of your energy and money, I could do this research that might uncover a wholly new energy source that would address some of the issues raised by peak oil and climate change." But you have invested everything already, so you have nothing to give. A possibility that might have made a difference goes unfunded by you.

This is describing a complex subtle energy phenomenon in a very simplistic way, but what it means is that the future is unfolding holistically, not along one single track alone. While there are those who are taking steps to prepare for the effects of peak oil and climate change, there are also those who are exploring new directions in science and technology, those who are seeking to bring about a change in consciousness within humanity, those who are working for governmental change, for social justice, for peace on earth, and there are those who are trying to maintain the status quo or at least get as much as they can from it before it goes bust. There are a lot of different people contributing in different ways with different visions to the future. They are all part of the larger landscape that I called the ecology of time. They are not all equal in motives, in power, or in effect, but they are all adding to the pot. It can make for a very muddled stew.

For many years I've taught classes in manifestation, which is a way of shaping one's personal future. I took the principles and insights I've learned in the process and turned them into visual aids in the form of a manifestation card deck and manual called *Manifestation: Creating the Life You Love*. My approach is different from the more familiar method of visualization, affirmation and positive thinking. I view manifestation as an aspect of the incarnational process and as such is as much about being as about getting.

Part of the process I teach is to look at what it is you want to manifest and then determine how it is connected in the world—which is to say, if you manifest this desire, what else comes with it, since nothing exists in a vacuum—and what is its essence. This latter is particularly important because often what a person says he or she wants to manifest isn't actually it. It may represent a deeper need or desire that could be satisfied in a number of different ways.

The future is essentially a manifestation project for humanity, one in which we are all engaged. Specific images of the future are like the form of that which we wish to manifest. But underneath them is a deeper condition that is what we are really trying to manifest. It may be that we get what we want but not in the form that we expected it to come; how will I recognize it if this happens if all I've been focused on is the form and not its essence?

Here's an example. A young man was trying to manifest a car that he could drive to work as bus service was erratic and undependable where he lived. He was not having any luck, however, so he came to talk with me about it. We used the card deck to work through the process. The form of what he wanted was a car. However, the connections that came with a car—the pattern that it formed with the world—was not something he appreciated. He was a dedicated environmentalist and hated the effect cars had on the world. And cars were part of a larger pattern that involved the petroleum industry, the tire industry, the road building industry, government (in the form of licensing), insurance companies, the need for parking space, the need for maintenance, and so on. If he manifested a car, he also manifested all these other connections into his life as well, none of which he wanted or appreciated.

The next card in the sequence asked him to determine the "heart" or the essence of what he was trying to manifest. He hadn't thought about this, but as he considered it, he realized that what he really wanted to manifest was transportation. He simply had assumed that it had to be a car, but now he realized that given his feelings of antipathy for automobiles and the whole infrastructure that supported them, it was no wonder he hadn't been able to manifest one. He would shift his focus to manifesting "transportation."

The next day he got in touch with me and said a friend of his had called him that morning to tell him he'd been reassigned out of the country, that he had a bike he couldn't take with him, and would he like it? His friend offered it to him as a gift. He had manifested his transportation in less than twenty-four hours, and the bike fit all his needs and desires and even some he hadn't known he had.

What really is the essence of the future humanity is trying to manifest? It's not really a "high-tech future" or a "low-tech future;" it's not any *image* of the future. Instead what we're trying to manifest are qualities such as safety, the ability to discover and express our human potentials, love, community, the ongoing fulfillment of what it means to be human, and so forth.

Peak oil or climate change doesn't lessen us as people. The type of future that unfolds need not limit our human qualities. My teen years were impoverished; my dad was unemployed for several years. Our dining room table was a wooden door supported by boxes, and my bed was a mattress on boxes, too. But those years were happy ones, with good friends, loving parents, and a wonderful world I was exploring. I had few of the things my classmates in high school had, but I didn't feel any less because of it. I didn't feel constricted or diminished. I didn't even feel poor, although I was.

Peak oil and climate change are not exactly images of the future; they are conditions in the world that have consequences that can shape the future, and thus out of them images arise. My point, born of my experience with manifestation, is to accept an image to work with and guide your life but don't become fixated upon it. Try to understand and support the underlying essence. A person creating a transition town community is trying to ensure that we have a good future in the midst of the consequences of diminishing resources and climate change. This may be a course you want to follow as well. But in doing so remember that a scientist working in the lab to create breakthroughs in alternative energy systems, or one working with bioengineering and genetics to craft food crops that can thrive in higher temperatures or in more strenuous conditions is working for the future, too.

Behind all the consequential futures and all the efforts to shape the future there is a presence of human creativity and beingness. We don't know the full power or capacity of this presence because we've never yet experienced it in the physical world; as a species we've been too fragmented, too conflicted, too divided. But this presence is still there and it is pushing for a future that allows it to express its wholeness.

I don't have the wisdom to know which images of the future will do that. A pragmatist will say, go for the images that promise survival, but which ones are those? Stewart Brand has a different set of pragmatic images than, say, John Michael Greer does, and both can marshal excellent and compelling evidence to support their positions.

So my approach of engagement is to accept both, to honor both, and in so doing to reach more deeply to honor the human striving and the spirit of humanity that is present in both these gentlemen and their work for what I think they would each acknowledge about the other—and which I can see in both of them—is that they each have a genuine love and caring for the wellbeing of the human race and of all the lives that share this world with us.

When you pick the future you want to believe in, support, work towards, and give your energy to, do all you feel is necessary to manifest it. But at the same time, open your heart and mind to some other alternatives, too. Not as a backup, not as a way of hedging your bets, and not because you feel unable to commit to any direction, but because one image is not sufficient to grasp the deeper essence of what is trying to unfold within humanity. One image is not a big enough tent to hold all the diverse creative imaginations, efforts, and styles that make up humanity. One image is not enough to let me attune to that deeper place where humanity itself as a collective presence struggles to be whole and to express its will within the ecology of time.

Humanity as a collective presence is trying to incarnate itself — manifest itself — in a way that fulfills both its innate potentials and those of the world of which it is a part. It seeks self-expression in a connected and holistic way. This holopoietic intent is then refracted and expressed through billions of individual people, each of whom interprets it through the lens of his or her individuality, where it becomes entwined with that person's desire to do the same thing on an individual level. The collective intent can be lost in the intensity of the individual desire, but as a person becomes more whole, more connected, more attuned and able to act beyond his or her personal interests, this collective energy comes to the fore and can make itself known. What future will serve not only my personal wellbeing but the wellbeing of all beings upon the earth? The more I can feel the intent of the human collective — what I call the Soul of Humanity — the more real and compelling this question becomes.

But ironically, the more I feel into this deeper, more holistic spirit, the more I realize that any individual image of the future that any person or group of persons comes up with is going to be incomplete; in its form, it can only capture part of the human experience, part of the human longing and creativity. The preferred future of an ecologist and environmentalist may not have room in it for the life's work and expression of a technologist or engineer and vice versa. The future of someone who loves cities may not match that of someone who loves the country.

Humanity needs its environmentalists and its technocrats, its urbanites and its rural folks because each of them embodies and expresses some facet of the whole human potential. The future we create or allow to unfold must have room for the whole of our humanity, not just for the parts we prefer or understand.

So in my own thinking of the future, I embrace and hold images that cater to the ecologist, the environmentalist, and the nature-oriented person, images that have a place for the scientist, the technician, the inventor, the engineer, images that have a place for the community person, the teller of tales, the weaver of relationships, and so forth. In this way, I try to practice a deeper attunement to the image of humanity itself engaged with its future. I take practical steps to foster the specific image to which I feel attuned (I'm a builder of relationships and one who works to foster a new consciousness), but I honor and support energetically those whose calling is different and who are guided by images of the future other than my own.

This idea of energetic support may seem strange and unfamiliar in our materialistic society. What does it mean to support something "energetically" or with subtle energies? The basic idea is not new at all; it underlies practices of prayer, blessing, "sending good thoughts," holding someone "in your heart," and so on. This idea is based on the concept that the world has a physical and a non-physical (or "subtle") side. Every person, every location, every situation generates a field of energy of some degree, shape and intensity that exists in the non-physical dimension of the world. These fields can be connected and linked just as people can be connected and linked, except that in the subtle worlds distance is no object. There is no separation due to space, only due to differences in energy. (An excellent exploration of use of these fields in education is Christopher Bache's book *The Living Classroom*. Another, more general book is *The Field*, by Lynn McTaggert.)

Working with these fields, generating them, linking them, sending energy between them can build pathways of thought, intention and vital, creative forces using the phenomenon of

"Gaianplasticity," roughly analogous to neuroplasticity, as I have said. The principle and art of doing so is called *subtle activism*.

The exploration of the connection between thought, intent and subtle forces in the world has been going on for millennia in one way or another, but it was brought to the attention of the public in another book by Lynn McTaggert, *The Intention Experiment*. More recently, even more work in this area is being done at The California Institute of Integral Studies, a university located in San Francisco. As an institution CIIS is known both for its intellectual rigor and its willingness to push the boundaries of academic exploration. It is famous for cutting-edge doctoral programs in holistic systems, transpersonal psychology, and transdisciplinary studies as well as the more traditional academic fare.

One of its professors, Dr. Sean Kelly, is a researcher in the field of subtle activism and has written scholarly papers on the topic. Along with David Nicol and Leslie Meehan, he has co-founded the Gaiafield Center for Subtle Activism at CIIS and launched the Gaiafield Project through an associated website, http://gaiafield.net. This project is one of both exploring the nature and dynamics of subtle activism and sponsoring subtle activism projects, usually involving large numbers of people in group meditation or prayer. The Gaiafield Project website defines subtle activism in this way:

> *Subtle Activism is an activity of consciousness or spirit, such as prayer, meditation, or ecstatic dance, intended to support collective healing and social change. Subtle Activism grows from the idea that there are many effective ways – some newly emerging, many as old as humanity – to positively influence social change other than overt political action....A global meditation and prayer event, in which hundreds of thousands of people around the planet unite in silence and prayers for world peace, is a prime example of subtle activism.*

Whereas Sean, David and Leslie are working with collective subtle activism, I explore and teach it at an individual level. How do we use our own subtle energies and the fields around us to engage with the world in beneficial and helpful ways?

The fields that surround us are both fields of vitality and life, thought and feeling, but also fields of probability. In a sense we are all always manifesting ourselves all the time, and at any given moment, certain patterns have a higher probability of becoming part of our life and incarnation than others. This process is also going on in the world at large. When viewed from the subtle realms, the world is a dynamic gradient of energies and patterns in various degrees of probability. It is possible to look at a person, for instance, and see not only who and what he or she is right now, but some of the echoes or energetic remnants of who he or she could have been or, in the other direction, some of the probabilities of who he or she may become in the future.

One form of subtle activism, though one to be practiced with great care and sensitivity, is to engage with a person's probability fields to shift the odds, so to speak, from one possible manifestation to another. (In effect, this is what the manifestation process I teach does but for oneself.) This can give rise to what I think of as partnering or collaborative subtle activism, something we can do as a way to engage the future.

Here are a couple of examples of what I mean. Let's go back to the idea of the BloomBox, or more generally to the possibility that an energy technology can be found, probably using the principles of distributive generativity, that can be clean, cheap, accessible, and able to be implemented in a world of increasing resource constraints. Somewhere in the world there are individuals—scientists, engineers, business people—who are seeking to make this possible not simply for individual gain but because they understand the situation humanity is in and want to help. They want to make it possible for humanity to continue to connect, form creative relationships, and unfold its potential. In one way or another, they are responding in their fashion to the creative presence of the future within the heart and Soul of humanity.

A simple subtle activism exercise is to take a moment to attune to your own field of incarnation and to find in yourself your connection to that holopoietic source, the life and intent of the Soul of Humanity within me. You can picture this, if you'd like, as a surge of radiance and Light in your own surrounding energy field, a heightening of your capacity to bless. Then you can picture in your imagination a person who stands as proxy for everyone who is conducting research in the field of alternative energy or you can picture a whole group of interrelated people—technicians, scientists, engineers, and so on—connected with this research. You then surround them with your own subtle field, which is connected to the Soul of Humanity, and use that as a catalyst to heighten their own connection to that larger presence and to heighten as well the probabilities within the energy field of their work that a solution may be found.

You can do exactly the same thing by picturing someone working to prepare for the effects of peak oil or climate change, perhaps a person organizing a transition torn or a person convening and hosting a World Café. Just follow the same procedure as above, using your own field as a catalyst and connection to enhance their efforts.

I may wholly believe that there is no alternative energy solution possible to civilization's energy crisis and that the most creative and constructive thing we can do is develop resilience in our local communities, plan for a world of Nineteenth-century technology, and adjust to a life-style equivalent to that in a modern third-world country. I may see that as a good thing because I am convinced that modern technological society is a blight upon the earth and a crushing weight upon humanity. But when I attune to the Soul of Humanity, I leave that behind. It's not that the Soul of Humanity rejects that possible outcome but that it doesn't represent the whole range of potentialities. In the act of subtle activism, I go to a place where I seek to empower all that range and those who seek to serve in ways different and with visions different from my own.

The same would be true if I feel that science and technology are the hope for the future, that we want to increase, not decrease, our technological prowess. I may choose to work to help bring that future about, but when I enter into the place from which I do this subtle activism, I embrace and seek to empower those who are working with transition towns and rural communities and the rediscovery of blacksmithing skills as much as those who are planning the latest generation of nuclear energy plants and BloomBoxes or their equivalents.

In a sense, we each need to forgive each other for our different images of the future! Or rather, more precisely, we need to forgive our tendency to say that our image is the inevitable image and everyone else needs to hop on board.

In this process, we are partnering with the future, but not with a specific future. We are partnering with the power of the future itself as a presence within us. As I suggested in talking about the ecology of time, the future is like a presence in its own right, an energy source in its own right, quite apart from any particular forms that future may take. It calls us out of the known, out of the familiar and into a place where only imagination, courage, and openness may take us.

It's good to have one or two consequential or specific images of the future that we align with that can guide our practical actions in the world, but we also want to practice our imagination of the future. We want to explore "what if....."

In that openness to "what if" we discover the power that makes us truly human and that is our greatest contribution to Gaia. We can be wildly imaginative and most of what we think of or come up with will have no chance of manifesting, but in the process we may find that one thought, that one insight, that one inspiration that can change everything. People have done it in the past. They will continue to do it in the future. There's no reason you can't be one of them.

Likewise, practice just being the creative future, going to that open, mysterious, unformed place of potential and feeling what that's like. No images, no forms, just a pure spirit of possibility. It can be an antidote to premature crystallization around a single image, a single possibility.

When our children were young, we used to take them to the Seattle Center where the world-famous Space Needle rises over the city and offers a panoramic view of the Puget Sound, the mountain ranges to the east and west, and the volcanoes of Mt. Baker to the north and Mt. Rainier to the south. Seattle Center is a collection of museums, theaters, art galleries, rides and restaurants.

One destination in particular for us was Center House where the Children's Museum was located. There were all kinds of interesting interactive displays to keep our kids occupied for hours, and one of the most popular was the Lego room.

This was simply a large room filled with hundreds and hundreds of Legos all scattered about the floor and room to build things. Here you could sit for hours, playing and building towers and bridges, cities and space ports, whatever you could imagine and could find a piece for.

The future for me is like that Lego room. It's not a set thing that's coming to us from around the bend like a package about to be delivered by Fed Ex or UPS. It's something emerging, something we're constructing day by day through our choices and actions. These choices cause some Lego shapes and pieces to disappear or to become scarce and introduce others into the mix, but we're still all sitting on the floor, putting our tomorrows together.

The future looms before us, but it is also spread out around us, waiting for us to play.

Chapter Thirteen
Day by Day

In this book, I've been talking about the long-range future of humanity. When people ask me about the future, this is usually what they mean, not their personal future in their individual lives. But we live in both kinds of time, collective time that we all experience together and personal time that only we experience individually. The two are deeply intertwined, of course. When the terrorists struck the World Trade Towers in 2001, it affected all of us across the United States and around the world. It was an event in our collective time and experience. But for the people in those buildings and their families, it was a tragic event in their personal time. I had a class two nights after that attack, and during it a woman shared her grief with the rest of us; she worked for a company whose headquarters had been in one of the Towers and several of her friends had been killed in that attack. For her the event was very personal.

So personal and collective time weave in and out of each other, each affecting the other. The same is true for our personal and collective futures. When I think of the future, I may think of how I'm going to pay my bills by the end of the month or I may think of how humanity will meet the challenges of climate change. One feels immediate and personal, the other feels more abstract and diffused. The bills lie on my desk, climate change lies on my mind, at least until or unless it manifests it some direct way for me.

Part of strategy for facing the future lies in bringing these two futures together. Here's a story from my time as co-director of the Findhorn Foundation community that will illustrate what I mean.

When I first arrived in the community in 1970 it was still a small group with only about fifteen or so residents. Its focus was on the garden and on preparing for a New Age. Like so many other New Age groups at the time, the New Age was an image of the future. It was something that was coming, but first there would be some great change on the earth. The founders of Findhorn were not apocalyptic in their thinking, but like most people in the New Age movement in those days, they saw they still assumed that something needed to happen in the world that would change people's attitudes and thinking and bring the New Age into being.

My own inner contact with John and his colleagues in the subtle worlds, though, gave me a different perspective. For them—and for me—the New Age was not an event but a state of mind; it was not a future but a way of creating the future. This attitude had been strengthened and affirmed for me by all the creative ferment in California where I lived, as I described in an earlier chapter. In short, for me the New Age was a consciousness that lived in us now and therefore could be expressed immediately. No waiting was required.

When I shared that perspective with Peter Caddy, he grasped immediately how transformative that idea could be. Like the manifestation exercise I described earlier, it separated the New Age out into its form and its essence. No one really knew—or could know—just what its form might be; that would evolve out of many sources over time. But the essence of the New Age, the spirit of the world that we hoped and envisioned would unfold, was much more clear. It was an expression of a holistic awareness, of love, of caring for each other and for the earth, of connectedness. We might not know fully all that this consciousness might express, but we knew the starting points. As I said to Peter at the time, "Whatever the New Age brings in the way of new forms of society, we still have to eat, we still have to raise food, we still have to work with each other, we still have to raise our children, we still have to love each other. It doesn't matter whether Findhorn is a 'New Age' community or an ordinary community. The basic human values and needs we need to express remain the same, and we can express those right now."

Out of this conversation, we determined that Findhorn was no longer waiting for a New Age but was being the New Age right now. We were collapsing a possible future into an immediate present. This might sound presumptuous but it meant that we could begin expressing the essence of the New Age in spirit and consciousness in a way that was creative. Simply saying "we are New Age" rather than "we will be New Age" made a big difference in approach. It made the abstract idea of a "New Age" existing in the collective future real and tangible—and accessible—in everyone's personal future, and more importantly, in everyone's present. This liberated an immense amount of vitality and creativity in the community.

In the last chapter, I suggested you hold in your heart and loving energy more than one image of the future. By so doing, you can go beyond their differences and similarities to attune to an underlying spirit. I think of that spirit as the Soul of Humanity seeking to unfold through any and all of our possible futures. While in many important ways the form the collective future will take is important and will make a difference in the lives and personal futures of billions of individual people, in another way it doesn't matter. There are basic human qualities that need and seek to be expressed whether the population of the earth is measured in thousands or in billions, whether we have the technology of 19th Century America or of the 23rd Century Federation in *Star Trek*. There are values in being human and in relating to each other and to the living world around us that hold true and need to be manifested whatever the future looks like. Those values don't need a future to come in order for us to understand and express them. We can do so right now, day by day. And there may be specific values peculiar to a particular expectation or image of the future that I can implement right now as well.

For instance, if I believe that we are in a process of deindustrialization due to the progressive loss of cheap fuel and energy, then values like frugality, conservation, self-reliance, and mutual support become important to survive and navigate such a future. But these are not values limited only to one kind of future; I can be frugal and conserve in a high-tech future and being willing to help and support others is always a timely virtue. Further, they are values I can express in my life now. I don't have to wait for a peak oil future to fully arrive in order to be frugal or conserving in my life or to learn skills that make me more self-reliant and so forth. And certainly nothing now stops me from reaching out to friends and neighbors and even strangers in my local area to form mutually helpful associations.

The values of a Peak Oil future are those I can live now day by day.

However, there is a word of caution here. We want to live our values and support each other not only or simply because they help us prepare for a particular future but because they are good values in themselves. If I am your neighbor, I would like to feel that you solicit a friendship with me because you're genuinely interested in who I am and have respect and care for me as a unique human being rather than feeling that you're making nice only so that I can be helpful and support you in a time of crisis.

In other words, the values that express our humanity at its best are there because of who we are, not because of where we might be going.

Peak Oil and climate change are not, strictly speaking, images of the future. They are, as I have said previously, images of conditions that are, in the ecology of time, contributing to the future that is unfolding. They are consequential futures, not ones that anyone is choosing and creating because they want to see a world where much of the land is either flooded or turned into a desert (in the worst case scenarios) or bereft of any of the higher technologies that now enable many of us to participate in a global culture. They are conditions to which we need to adapt, and it's the various possible adaptations that actually form the various images of the future that people are imagining and for which they are planning.

But in all cases, this adaptation depends on the wise and skilled expression of basic human values that we want to express anyway: values of love, mutual regard, cooperation, community, non-violent communication, and so on. Again, my expression of these values doesn't depend on what my image of the future may be.

When my son John-Michael, who is twenty-seven years old, sent me the email telling me about Bloom Energy and the BloomBoxes, he added in passing, "I love the idea of our future!" Although Johnny is conversant with all of the images of the future I've discussed in this book and with the problems of peak oil and climate change, he firmly believes that the actual future that unfolds will be wonderful. He has no fears for tomorrow. He is positive about what humanity can and will do. He loves and enjoys people and consequently, like many of his generation, he is totally immersed in the social networking possibilities that modern wireless computer technology can offer.

But when I think of Johnny, I don't see someone who is dedicated to a technological future. What I see is someone who is open to discovery and the excitement of life. He is open to possibilities. His imagination is open to the world and especially to other people. For him, the saying that there are no strangers, only friends I haven't met yet is absolutely true. This would be true for him whatever form the future takes.

This is a generality for which there are many exceptions. But on the whole, when I've conversed with people who see our future shaped by Peak Oil and climate change, I usually find them constricted in their energy and imaginations. They are imagining a constricted world, so they are already taking on its characteristics. Conversely, when I've been around engineers and people in love with gadgets who see a bright technological future ahead (which would describe my second son, Aidan who like his grandfather and great-grandfather before him, is training to be an engineer), I often find them open, expansive, and positive in their imaginations. They see a future filled with possibilities and the overcoming of limits, and this reflects itself in how they express themselves and a feeling of personal creativity.

As I said, this is a very generalized statement. I know expansive, open, imaginative, positive people who have no doubt that industrial civilization is on its way out, and constricted, pessimistic, isolated people who have no doubt technology will solve everything. My point is not that one image of the future makes us one way and another image makes us a different way. In fact, my native disposition and character—such as whether I'm fundamentally an optimist or a pessimist—may determine what image of the future attracts me and in which I end up believing. My point is that whatever image of the future we hold can shape how we engage with the present. We end up living our futures in our attitudes day by day long before they actually manifest in time.

I happen to believe strongly in the necessity and value of boundaries and membranes; they are a vital part of the incarnational process. Limits are good things, not restrictions, for they shape and channel energy and consciousness in meaningful and precise ways, allowing individuality to manifest. But I also believe in spaciousness and in the expansiveness of life. It's a paradox, but a key one, the relationship between order and chaos, the fixed and the fluid, limits and growth on which all life depends. In a way our images of the future reflect this paradox: some focus on limits, some focus on growth. From my point of view, it's not an either/or relationship. We need both.

This is one reason I rejoice in having both the vision of a future with limits as dictated by peak oil and climate change and a future of growth and expansion as reflected in technological and scientific optimism. I want to hold both of them in a tension within me and discover the deeper life that resonates between them. It's from this deeper place, within the ecology of time, that the future we experience will undoubtedly come, a future that has, as all life does, both limits and growth, both order and chaos.

When someone comes to me and asks, "Are we going to have a bleak future," one response I have is, "Are you having a bleak present?" I remember well a woman who came to me back in the Sixties who had been reading about a particularly violent, apocalyptic prophecy that was making the rounds then. She was very fearful as she talked to me, and I assumed she was fearful about what would happen if the prophecy came to pass. But as it turned out, I was wrong. She was fearful that the apocalypse wouldn't happen. "I have a dead end job and a loveless marriage," she said. "I know this event would change all that, but I'm afraid it won't happen!"

She felt constricted in her life and unable to break out using her own capabilities. In response, she felt drawn to a constricted (though oddly liberating) image of the future in which millions of people would die in earth changes and human civilization would be destroyed.

There is no bleak future, for the future hasn't happened yet, and when it does, I may find it has more possibilities that I imagined, even though its form may be constricted and limiting in a variety of ways. Likewise, there is no positive future, for the same reason; when a future I imagined as being positive comes into being, I may discover it has a dark, limiting, distressing side that I had not anticipated. In fact, that's precisely what we're experiencing now in Western culture. The abundant technological society we enjoy in the industrialized nations fulfills the dreams and wishes of many of our ancestors and on the surface looks like the positive, utopian, golden ages of their legends. We have safety from the ravages of nature, we have abundant food, we have medical services that can keep us healthy for many years, we have riches of clothing, entertainment, transportation, and the like that the most powerful kings and emperors of the past could never have enjoyed. And yet, we see how the industrial and technological capabilities that have brought us these things are damaging the earth, destroying eco-systems, creating pressure and stress, and give us weapons that can kill billions and even wipe out all life on earth. A positive future has in some ways shown itself to be very negative.

. Each day presents me with opportunities for kindness, for positive interactions with people, for loving interaction with my world, and with a chance to increase the store of happiness in the world. I don't want to miss those opportunities in my day by day world because of the images I hold for my future world. Whatever its form, I want the future to continue those opportunities and to expand them as well; that's true whether I have to travel by stagecoach or train or by jet and spacecraft. Any future has a greater chance to become a positive one if I embody and live a positive present in the connections and relationships I form right now.

How do I face and engage with the future? Through what I embody in the present, one day at a time.

Chapter Fourteen
School Kids

I am optimistic about the future. In spite of all the scary images of what can happen or may happen, I believe humanity is on the right track. One reason for that, as I have already mentioned, is because of my relationship to the subtle worlds and my awareness of all that they do to help us. Humanity is getting a great deal of help to make it through the coming years, and we have the capacity within us to rise to the occasion and create a holistic civilization that truly serves us and all life upon this world. Why should we settle for less?

There's another reason why I'm optimistic. It comes from an odd experience I had a number of years ago.

One day I found myself in touch with beings of a totally different nature than any I had contacted before. Instead of being intelligences living in the subtle realms of the earth, these were two individuals who seemed to be living in the future.

The whole feel of this encounter was different from anything I had experienced before. It felt like two different personalities were looking out at the world through my eyes, each discussing what they were seeing with each other. Unlike a contact with a spiritual or non-physical being which carries for me a distinctive and discernable "feel" that engages my whole being, this had a purely mental flavor to it, as if I were in telepathic contact with two physical individuals living not only elsewhere on the earth but as it turned out, *elsewhen*.

If this sounds like something out of science fiction (or the insane asylum), it's actually not an unheard of phenomenon. It's been a recognized part of the shamanic tradition for thousands of years that a person may, through dreams or trance or some other method, find himself or herself contacting the mind of a descendent in the future or an ancestor in the past. I knew that this could take place, and a friend of mine, Robert Moss, has written an excellent book, *Dreamways of the Iroquois*, based on this phenomenon. However, it had never happened to me before.

This experience did not take place in any kind of altered state of consciousness. It happened one day as I was walking down the streets of a city near where I live. I became aware of presences in my mind—I have no other way to describe it—as if I were overhearing their conversation telepathically. They were seeing what I was seeing, and they were marveling at it. The feeling of excitement and wonder that they were sharing was amusing and delightful to me, like seeing the awe on my kids' faces when my wife and I first took them to Disneyland. I had the impression that these two individuals were like anthropology students from the future taking a telepathic field trip into the past to do research and for some reason had linked up with my mind. Perhaps they were descendents of mine.

They were studying everything around me as if it were ancient history to them, a world out of the mists of legend. I imagined I would feel exactly the same if I suddenly found myself looking through the eyes of a citizen in Rome when Augustus was Caesar or walking through London during the reign of Elizabeth the First. I remember very well their excitement at seeing cars on the road and one exclaiming, "You see, they really were powered by internal combustion engines!"

To say this was a strange experience is putting it mildly, but I found myself caught up in their enthusiasm. The contact never lasted long at any one time, at first no more than five to ten minutes and later maybe twenty minutes to half an hour at the most, but it happened frequently over a period of about a year. At first I was like a bystander to them, as if their telepathic perception—however they were doing it—bypassed my consciousness (though it wasn't like they controlled my mind or body or anything spooky like that), but gradually we began to talk to each other. Because they could only see what I was looking at, they would occasionally ask me to look right or left or to go into a particular building so they could see something. I felt as if they were graduate students doing research on the past for some term paper in a far future university.

As the contact developed, I became a willing partner with them. It was exciting. Like escorting visitors from out of town, it was an opportunity to see familiar sites in a fresh way. They asked me once to drive around so they could see the city where I live from a variety of vantage points, which I was happy to do, and they were fascinated by everything they saw. In particular, they were fascinated by automobiles. Their feeling was like I might have seeing an ancient chariot. "They have not existed for a long time," one of them said. "They're a primitive mode of transportation that damaged the earth."

Needless to say, after the first two or three visits, when I realized this was not some strange passing phenomenon or a bout of indigestion, I tried to question them. What was their world like? How far in the future were they? What lay ahead for us in our future? I felt particularly prompted to enquire because they kept saying things like, "See? This is what the world was like before the Change," and I could hear the capital "C" in their thoughts.

They tried to answer me as best they could, but it was hard. Whatever the method was that they were using, they could receive from me more easily than they could transmit. But the real challenge, I came to understand, was that they didn't have all the answers to my questions. They really did feel to me like students or young people who took their own world for granted, who hadn't thought about it much and didn't know much about its history. Indeed, their exploration into our time seemed part of their learning. I could imagine if a Roman citizen from the first century CE asked a typical American high school student to describe the two thousand years of history separating them from him and to tell him about the politics, culture, and science of our world. Most of them would be unable to do it and would instead probably talk about shopping malls, Ipods, and hip hop music.

It was this sense from them of the ordinariness of their world, how much they took it for granted, and how little they really knew about it that gave the whole experience a sense of verisimilitude for me. This wasn't some grand high visitor from the future come to give me a message or provide insights into the times to come; these were like kids out on a field trip, wonderfully and perhaps unexpectedly connecting telepathically with some guy, perhaps a distant ancestor, in their ancient past. Cool!

But there were images that they were able to convey. From their perspective, they lived in a peaceful world. I had the impression that the world population was not as large as it is today, but that may have been due to their living in an area of fewer people. They lived in a sophisticated technological society, but the glimmers that I caught about that technology in their thoughts made it seem psychic or mental in nature, almost what we might call "magical" (keeping in mind Clarke's Law—one of three "laws of prediction" formulated by science fiction writer and futurist, Arthur C. Clarke—which states that "any sufficiently advanced technology is indistinguishable from magic"). One thing for sure: they didn't have internal combustion engines or cars!

The one image that was dominant, though, was that their civilization was profoundly connected to water. I came to realize they meant this in two ways. The first was that the culture these two came from was a maritime culture and that their world had a good deal more water in it than ours does. Land masses were smaller than in our day. In fact, they themselves seemed to be living in what now is Australia or at least in the South Pacific. Apparently at some time between our time and theirs, the sea level had significantly risen.

The second was that much of their technology was based on water and drew its energy from water. I had the impression that this was true both for the physical energy, such as electricity, that powered their society, and for the metaphysical or "psychic" energy which they used as well.

The earth itself seemed to be a partner in their culture. They took the livingness of the planet for granted and were surprised that people in my time did not ("but remember," one said, "this was before the Change").

And how far in the future were they? They didn't know. They

didn't seem to understand my sense of time or use of calendars and dates. At least they didn't date things the way we do. It was far enough ahead that we were something of a distant memory, a time of legend but not so far ahead that we were forgotten. I had the sense there were still connections between their world and ours, some technologies perhaps, some customs, even language, probably some cities that were still around, like Rome is for us. If I were to guess, and it would only be a guess, I might say they came from three to four hundred years in our future.

And there was a clear sense that between their world and ours, a Change had occurred. Part of this Change apparently had been destructive, as one might imagine if the sea levels rose significantly, but part of it had come about through other means, through discoveries and through shifts in consciousness. They were not explicit and I'm not sure they even knew fully what it was, any more than the average teenager could describe in detail for you what the Renaissance was or the Industrial Revolution.

Mostly what I gained from them was the sense of a clean, beautiful world, simpler in some ways but more advanced in other ways than ours, a world in which humanity and the earth had both come to a safe and relatively happy place. Perhaps most telling was the almost unconscious sense of pride both my visitors had, something they didn't talk about but which I could feel in their presence. This was not pride in dominating their world but pride in being a loving and contributing part of a larger wholeness. They were proud at being human but they defined their humanity in terms of partnering with the rest of the natural world, not in trying to control it.

This contact was a sporadic one that lasted about a year, and then they vanished. I've never heard from them since. Were they really from the future? I don't know. That was my sense of it, but maybe they came from one of many possible futures. When dealing with these kind of phenomena, it's best not to draw hard and fast conclusions but to allow space for a bit of mystery, a bit of wonder and speculation.

However, that's not the end of the story. In the years since I had that experience, I've thought about the vision of their world that the two visitors had given me and about a technology that could draw both physical and psychic energies from water. Then I came across an article about Daniel Nocera, a chemist at MIT, who has discovered a way to make hydrogen fuel directly from water at room temperature using means akin to the photosynthetic processes in plants which can split water into hydrogen and oxygen using sunlight. Reading this and then doing some research on the Internet about Nocera and his process, I was struck by the fact that here potentially was a simple, cheap way to produce and store energy using water, exactly the kind of technology that my visitors from the future had said was a cornerstone of their civilization.

While this information doesn't prove my contact, nonetheless in reading of Nocera's work I felt affirmed in the validity of my experience. At the very least, a water-based energy technology for society of the kind I had been told about was a real possibility.

What is even more exciting to me about this is that this possible technology is coming into being by paying attention to and learning from the natural processes of photosynthesis. Essentially Nocera's work is based on doing what plants do. That was his breakthrough insight. It is giving him success in an area where others have failed. I see this as an example of learning to think like a planet, to think with nature instead of against nature. This is exactly the kind of thinking that my inner sources have said is the objective of the "world project" I wrote about earlier. In its way it is a confirmation of the work that they are doing to inspire and promote exactly this kind of holistic thought.

It is also the kind of thinking that seemed to characterize the world my visitors came from. As far as I could tell from listening to them and from the "feel" of them, they came from a culture that quite naturally thought and acted in harmony with the world; they both had a love for the world that would not let them do otherwise. I could feel it as an underlying current. It made me realize that if we could think and act from that kind of love, we could transform our world and come to a good future.

Then, while preparing to write this book, I wrote to my friend, Lee Irwin, to ask him if he had any visions of the future. With his background of practice in mysticism, shamanism, and esotericism, Lee is one of the most deeply attuned people I know. He has a long history of contact with the subtle realms to which he brings the intellectual rigor of a professional scholar. He wrote me a long letter in reply and generously gave me permission to quote from it here.

I have a strange double vision, but the two halves do fit together. On the one hand, I see a very distinct loss of population, radically lower in the future than in the present, along with some significant earth changes, often linked with a dying out of old order political and religious beliefs and practices. However, in that future life is good, very good, the oceans are much higher and there is less land mass, there is far less industrialization and a more earth related culture but great technological sophistication. The 20-21st centuries are regarded as primitive times and not very well known, usually collapsed into the 18-19th centuries, and somewhat regarded with horror due to massive wars, overpopulation, technical predation, and lack of human concern for humanity and the earth.

On the other hand, I see an increasing wave of population growing considerably beyond the current population throughout the 21st century and creating massive stress and difficulty. At the same time there is an increasing loss of fertility among human beings that cannot be cured or "fixed" - a kind of planetary response to excessive population. During this period there is the discovery of a new and non-harmful energy source, something really amazing that completely changes the entire industrial base and leads to a sharp decline in the use of oil and coal and gas. Whatever it is, it is non-polluting, very powerful, commonly available, and once the technology is understood, incredibly adaptable – it may have something to do with anti-gravity – because I also see the development of anti-gravity devices as common and widely used. Another element here is a profoundly interconnected superweb for communication, almost indestructible and inexpensive computer devices, and some actual implantation of "nodes" in the human body for enhanced communication.

These two scenarios combine as follows: the population increases, technology develops, long life expectancy is balanced off against loss of fertility, at a certain point (unknown) the population crests and begins a radical decline, partly due to loss of fertility from overpopulation, partly due to earth changes (including a possible shift in the poles and a small ice age), and primarily due to a radical transformative event – the birthing of a shared planetary consciousness, a Gaia-field of immense vitality powered by the large mental-emotive awareness of our high population.

This is a cresting phenomena – the waves of consciousness sweep up everyone, but not everyone can integrate the intensity and scope of the waves – a percentage of the population is integrated into the new consciousness which includes paranormal perceptions and advanced psychic abilities, while a larger percentage experiences a profound expansion but then, cannot sustain participation in the new Gaiafield. This results in a backlash, some sporadic violence but then the overall effects of the great transformation begin to fade, leaving after the peak a residual consciousness in some that is carried forward with marked abilities that lead to a new social order on a global scale, though one that prioritizes local community over global relations.

A whole new technology develops based on psychic sciences and a "new physics" in which E=MC2 is based on "energy = matter + consciousness squared" (to speak metaphorically) and while the superweb collapses entirely and history is rewritten (so the 20-21st centuries are "primitive"), the new social order is able to sustain an expansive consciousness that participates in an expanded trans-gaiafield [that reaches into the cosmos.]

The question remains – will humanity take the path of higher transformation or through criminal actions, neglect, and predation, actually destroy or deny the profound spiritual potential that is our greatest gift? I fully believe that the innate power of Spirit is the foremost guide and inner creative power of this change and that human beings who fully embrace their spiritual potential become agents of transformation that will lead to a difficult, painful but successful rebirth in which we will collapse the inflation and confusion of current thinking into a far more integrated, spiritually deep realization of human potential.

And what will become of those who do not make the transition? Nothing, they simply won't see what can be seen, holding on to old myths, lesser visions, and nay-saying. What reproduces in a creative, dynamic universe of consciousness are those beings who hold the energies of change in a positive, loving, caring, wise manner – who help their brothers and sisters, regardless of their attitudes or denials, and who, inspired by moral clarity and deep commitment to positive change, become leaders and visionaries able to hold the vision and make it real.

The parallels between what Lee has seen in his own inner visions and the information my visitors gave me is striking. It doesn't prove anything, at least not in any scientific way, but I find it highly affirming and suggestive of one configuration at least of the landscape of time that surrounds us.

Not so long ago, I was meeting with a group of people whom I met at a conference. It was one of those casual gatherings between sessions, and the discussion had turned to how dark and hopeless the future seemed to many of the people there. I shared this story of my visitors with them, and I could feel the atmosphere of the group shift and relax.

"That's wonderful," one woman said.

"But I don't know," I replied, "if this experience was a contact with the actual future or a possible future, or something else entirely."

"It doesn't matter," she said. "It gives me hope, and that's what I need."

It gives me hope, too. Not necessarily because it's a prophecy, because I don't know if it's a true prophecy or not, though I value its positive vision. It gives me hope because of something else I felt from my two visitors.

They had a sophisticated technology, different from but equal to our own in many ways; they were certainly not primitives eking out bare survival from a blasted and devastated world. But the fundamental characteristic of their world was not its technology but its consciousness, the way people thought and felt about themselves and the planet. And in their discussions with each other, it became clear to me that the reason they wanted to visit and see our world and our time was that it was here and now that that consciousness began. The roots of their world were in ours. They were visiting what to them was the time from which their hopeful world emerged. For them, the beginning of that hope was in our present. We contain the seeds that will blossom into their world.

That is what gives me hope. Whether that future will exist or not, whether my visitors are real people or not, the possibilities that it could exist are very real right now. They are possibilities we can work with and explore. We are not prisoners of old consciousness or of habit. We can change our minds and our hearts. We can reach out to each other in friendship and collaboration and stand for a world that serves all life. We have capacities of love, imagination, creativity, and powers of partnership on which to draw. We can be Internauts, working with "Gaianplasticity," building the connections for a new world and shaping possibilities and probabilities into new forms and relationships. We can learn to think like a planet and we can act from that perspective.

I hope we do. If so, then somewhere in the future, in the vast ecology of time, there are two school kids writing a term paper that says their present began with us.

Resources

These resources are listed alphabetically by person. I include in parenthesis some key words that tie into concepts mentioned in the text. Wherever possible, under each person I've included both books they've written that are relevant to the text of Facing the Future and their website where more information is available. Please note that while books can last and be readily available, at least in libraries if not always on bookstore shelves, websites on the other hand are notorious for disappearing into cyberspace. All the websites listed below were active up to the time of publication, but this is no guarantee that they will always be there.

Christopher M. Bache (consciousness; subtle fields; subtle energies)
- Book: *The Living Classroom: Teaching and Collective Consciousness.* SUNY Press (2008)

Carolyn Baker (Peak Oil and Collapse)
- Book: *Sacred Demise: Walking the Spiritual Path of Industrial Civilization's Collapse.* iUniverse.com. (2009)
- Website: www.carolynbaker.net
   Articles recommended on her website:
      * When Facing Reality is Not Negative Thinking
      * Collapse Conundrum: Confrontation or Descent by Degrees
      * Humanity's Rite of Passage: A World Tended by Adults.

Sharon Begley (neuroplasticity; consciousness)
- Book: *Train Your Mind, Change Your Brain.* Ballantine Books (2007)

Resources

William Bloom (New Age; Consciousness Shift; Holistic Spirituality; Positive Future)
- Book: *Soulution*. Hay House (2004)
- Website: http://www.williambloom.com
- Website: http://www.f4hs.org

Teena Booth (New Age; Creating Positive Future)
- Book: *Unfinished Evolution*. Scotalyn Press (2009)
- Website: www.newagepride.org

Edmund J. Bourne (New Age; Consciousness Shift)
- Book: *Global Shift: How a New Worldview is Transforming Humanity*. New Harbinger (2009)
- Website: http://www.noetic.org

Steward Brand (positive futures)
- Book: *Whole Earth Discipline: An Ecopragmatist Manifesto*. Viking (2009)
- Website: http://web.me.com/stewartbrand/SB_homepage/Home.html

Juanita Brown with David Isaacs (positive futures; creating relationships; "world project")
- Book: *The World Café: Shaping Our Futures Through Conversations That Matter*. Berrett-Koehler (2005)
- Website: http://www.theworldcafe.com

Shaun Chamberlin (Peak Oil; Positive Future)
- Book: *The Transition Timeline: For a Local Resilient Future*. Chelsea Green Publishing (2009)
- Website: www.transitiontown.org

Vine Deloria (human capacities; spirituality; consciousness)
- Book: *The World We Used to Live In: Remembering the Power of the Medicine Men*. Fulcrum Publishing (2006)

Norman Dodge (neuroplasticity, consciousness)
- Book: *The Brain that Changes Itself*. Penguin (2007)

Stephan Faris (Climate Change)
- Book: *Forecast: The Surprising—and Immediate—Consequences of Climate Change*. Holt Paperbacks (2009).
- Website: http://www.stephanfaris.com

"JD" (anti-peak oil)
- Internet Blog: http://peakoildebunked.blogspot.com

Gaiafield Project (new consciousness, subtle activism, connections and community)
- Website: http://www.gaiafield.net

Greater Good Science Center (new consciousness, human capacities, science and the future)
- Website: http://peacecenter.berkeley.edu/index.html

John Michael Greer (Peak Oil)
- Book: *The Long Descent: A Users Guide to the End of the Industrial Age*. New Society Publishers. (2008)
- Book: *The Ecotechnic Future: Envisioning a Post-Peak World*. New Society Publishers. (2009)
- Website: http://thearchdruidreport.blogspot.com/
     Articles Recommended on his website:
         * The Coming of Deindustrial Society
         * The Long Road Down: Decline and the Deindustrial Future
         * Druidry and the Future
- Website: http://starsreach.blogspot.com/ (a science-fiction novel of a post-industrial world)

Resources

David Holmgren (Peak Oil and Collapse; Positive Future)
- Book: *Future Scenarios: How Communities Can Adapt to Peak Oil and Climate Change.* Chelsea Green Publishing. (2009)
- Book: *Permaculture: Principles and Pathways Beyond Sustainability.* Holmgren Design Services. (2002)

Rob Hopkins (Peak Oil and Collapse; Positive Future)
- Book: *The Transition Handbook: From Oil Dependency to Local Resilience.* Chelsea Green Publishing. (2008)
- Website: www.transitiontowns.org

Lee Irwin (Native American Prophecy; Spirituality)
- Book: *Coming Down From Above: Prophecy, Resistance and Renewal In Native American Religions.* University of Oklahoma Press. (2009)
- Book: *Visionary Worlds: The Making and Unmaking of Reality.* SUNY Press (1996)
- Book: *Alchemy of Soul.* Lorian Press (2007)

Phil Lane, Jr. (Indigenous Peoples, Planetary Consciousness)
- Website: http://www.fwii.net

Dorothy Maclean (Findhorn co-founder, attunement to the god within and nature intelligences)
- Book: *To Hear the Angels Sing* (Lorian Press 1980-2008)
- Website: http://www.lorian.org

Elizabeth Lloyd Mayer (human capacities; miracles; expanded consciousness)
- Book: *Extraordinary Knowing: Science, Skepticism, and the Inexplicable Powers of the Human Mind.* Bantam (2007)

Lynn McTaggart (human capacities, subtle activism, intentionality)
- Book: *The Field: The Quest for the Secret Force of the Universe.* Harper (2008)

- Book: *The Intention Experiment: Using Your Thoughts to Change Your Life and the World*. Free Press (2007)
- Website: http://www.theintentionexperiment.com

Robert Moss (Imagination and Dreaming)
- Book: *The Three "Only" Things*. New World Library (2009)
- Website: www.mossdreams.com

Belden Paulson (New Age Vision; Practical, Positive Futures)
- Book: *Odyssey of a Practical Visionary*. Thistlefield Books (2009)

John Perkins (Shaping the Future; Human Capabilities; Systemic dysfunction)
- Book: *The World is as You Dream It*. Destiny Books. (1994)
- Book: *Shapeshifting: Techniques for Global and Personal Transformation*. Destiny Books (1997)
- Book: *Confessions of an Economic Hit Man*. Plume (2005)
- Book: *Hoodwinked*. Broadway Business (2009)
- Website: www.dreamchange.org

Louis M. Savary and Patricia H.Berne (connections; consciousness)
- Book: *Kything: The Art of Spiritual Presence*. Paulist Press. (1989)

Daniel J. Siegel (transformation; neuroplasticity; consciousness)
- Book: *Mindsight: The New Science of Personal Transformation*. Bantam (2010)
- Website: http://www.mindsightinstitute.com

Rebecca Solnit (consciousness, positive futures, disasters, community)
- Book: *A Paradise Built in Hell: The Extraordinary Communities that Arise in Disaster*. Penguin (2009)

Resources

Lee Smolin (Living Universe)
- Book: *The Life of the Cosmos*. Oxford University Press. (1999)

David Spangler (Manifestation; Shaping the Future; Incarnational Spirituality; Subtle Worlds)
- Book and Manifestation Card Deck: *Manifestation: Creating the Life You Love*. Lorian Press (2004)
- Book: *Everyday Miracles*. Lorian Press (1996-2008)
- Book: *The Laws of Manifestation*. Weiser Books. (2009)
- Book: *Subtle Worlds: An Explorer's Field Notes*. Lorian Press (2010)
- Website: www.Lorian.org

Robert Stilger (Positive Futures; creating relationships; "world project")
- Book: *Enspirited Leadership: Creating a Future of Possibilities*. The Barkana Institute. (2005)
- Website: http://resilientcommunities.org
- Website: www.barkana.org

William Irwin Thompson (Images of the Future; Shaping the Future)
- Book: (with David Spangler as co-author) *Reimagination of the World: A Critique of the New Age, Science, and Popular Culture*. Bear and Co. (1991)
- Book: *Gaia: A Way of Knowing*. Lindisfarne Press (1988)
- Book: *Transforming History: A new Curriculum for a Planetary Culture*. Lindisfarne Press (2009)
- Website: www.williamirwinthompson.org
- Online Column: http://www.wildriverreview.com/Column/ Thinking_Otherwise/William_Irwin_Thompson/10_16_09

Trivedi Foundation (science, human capacities, expanded consciousness)
- Website: http://www.divinelifefoundation.us/default2. aspx?cid=36

Margaret Wheatley (consciousness; positive future; connections and relationships)
- Book: *Turning to One Another: Simple Conversations to Restore Hope to the Future*. Barrett-Koehler (2002)
- Website: http://www.margaretwheatley.com

Arthur Zajonc (consciousness, science, human capacities, connecting to the world; love)
- Book: *Meditation as Contemplative Inquiry: When Knowing Becomes Love*. Lindisfarne Press (2009)
- Website: http://www.arthurzajonc.org

Phil Zimbardo (consciousness, social change, human capacities, evil, heroism)
- Book: *The Lucifer Effect: Understanding How Good People Turn Evil*. Random House (2007)
- Website: http://www.lucifereffect.com/index.html
- Website: http://heroicimagination.org/ (the Heroic Imagination Project)

Resources

About the Publisher

Lorian Press is a private, for profit business which publishes works approved by the Lorian Association. Current titles by David Spangler and others can be found on the Lorian website.

Lorian Press
2204 E Grand Ave
Everett, WA 982901

About The Lorian Association

The Lorian Association is a not-for-profit educational organization. Its work is to help people bring the joy, healing, and blessing of their personal spirituality into their everyday lives. This spirituality unfolds out of their unique lives and relationships to Spirit, by whatever name or in whatever form that Spirit is recognized.
For information, go to www.lorian.org, email info@lorian.org, or write to:

The Lorian Association
P.O. Box 1368
Issaquah, WA 98027

LaVergne, TN USA
23 August 2010
194269LV00001B/3/P